A Small Journey Through *A Big World*

I AM

MORE

THAN WHAT YOU SEE

Sat /8 /2018

Thank you.

Remember that your Vision is the

RENALDO LAWRENCE

Most important thing. If you can see it,

RIlearning Ltd. *you can be it*

Renaldo Lawrence

Published by Rllearning Ltd.

Editing: Self Publish -N- 30 Days

Interior Design: Self Publish -N- 30 Days

Printed in the United States of America

ISBN: 978-1979931748

1. Self Help 2. Success-Psychological Aspects

Renaldo Lawrence: I AM MORE THAN WHAT YOU SEE

Dedicated to my parents and family.

The greatest gift we can give anyone is our gift of confirmation and love.
To affirm someone is to give them life. And to give life is giving someone permission
to feel good about themselves which can propel them to greatness.

ACKNOWLEDGEMENTS

I would like to thank everyone who helped me with this book, and the people who continued to encourage me to get it done, especially my mother who continually over the years put the thought in my mind about writing a book. I would like to thank the editors at the publishing company, family members who read or helped me to remember stories, friends who helped in any way and researchers. A big thanks to my wife, Janis, for always caring, and to my two wonderful children, Andrew and Jessica. Because of you guys, I'm allowed to breathe like I never could. Tyrone Sackiel, my brother, you have been a foundation in my life.

This book is also dedicated to a special friend, Kevin Cadle, whom the world lost on Monday 16th October 2017. My life will continue to be a reflection of the greatness you demonstrated with yours.

The one thing I know from living my life is this; it doesn't matter where you are or where you come from, it all starts with your ability to think yourself into a position of success. Whatever you believe, there is an amazing chance that you are right. The other necessities are that you chart your course through life by first believing in yourself, writing down your goals, and then planning a strategy to reach your goals through consistent work every day.

Life gives you very few guarantees, one is that you are going to die. So, while you have the unbelievable privilege to live on this planet, you owe it to yourself to try and be the best you can be daily. You make choices every day, and today you will set the path for your future, and there is only one person who can determine how amazing that journey will be, and that person is you. However, during your amazing journey, remember this;

I believe giving is a part of the reason we are all here, to give and help each other live an amazing life. Take the opportunity at every turn to give to someone so that we as a collective can prosper.

Good luck with your journey. You are as blessed as you make up your mind you want to be.

"No one ever became poor by giving."
—Anne Frank

CONTENTS

INTRODUCTION

When I look back over my life, there have been many times when I have thought of writing a book. I could count on 5 sets of hands the number of times my mother mentioned writing a book to me. It was only after I read a book called, *The Power of Now: A Guide to Spiritual Enlightenment*, by Eckhart Tolle, that I realized that yes, I do have a contribution to share with the world. And yes, I want to share my journey.

From reading the very first page of Eckhart Tolle's extraordinary book, I knew I had to write this book because I have a voice with something to say, which I thought would not only resonate with the world, but also share ideas and concepts which could help anyone become successful.

This book is ten years in the making. After years of not listening to my inner voice or anyone else's for that matter, my mother for one, I decided it was time. While I had really no idea what I was going to write, I thought the best and most direct approach was to write about events which occurred during my lifetime with a peek back through my history. I have always felt different all of my life, so the best way I believe I can start describing my life and feelings is to start with people who I have read about, people who I viewed as different or creative.

So here we go. If you look back through history, there are so many examples of people who have to be considered as different. Yet, these people have made such a difference in the world that it's still felt today. For example, we are still talking about the amazing composer called J. S. Bach, who during his lifetime was considered anything but a genius.

As a matter of fact, his music was considered a little old-fashioned for its time, enjoyed only by connoisseurs. The authorities at Leipzig famously complained that they only employed Bach because "the best [Telemann] was not available." Bach's principal reputation was not as a composer, but as an astonishingly gifted organ player and improviser, and a consultant for organ repair. It is amazing that today we think of him as one of the greatest composers the world has ever known. Look at how much we now love and adore him and his music. But it didn't start out that way at all.

Steve Jobs was considered very different by a lot of people, so much so that he was even fired from the company he founded. He went against the norm and created the first computer retail store of its kind in history. (Oh yes, he also created the iPhone.) These stores have sold and continue to sell so many devices that have helped make people's lives so much better.

On top of that, the stores allow customers to touch the devices without any hassle from the employees. You get a real sense of belonging when you visit an Apple store. So, in his own way, he changed the retail culture of our society.

Steve Jobs believed in his vision passionately. In the process of trying to express and live that vision, he created a landmark video 'Think Different' which won countless awards and radically changed the advertising industry. And to top it off, when he took over Apple again, yep, he was fired the first time around, it became the wealthiest company in the world, along the way delivering products which made people's lives simpler and easier, and which, quite frankly, changed the world.

Another amazing example is that of Madam C. J. Walker. Sarah Breedlove (December 23rd 1867 – May 25th 1919), known as Madam C. J. Walker, was an African American entrepreneur, philanthropist, a political and social activist. Do you think when she started as an entrepreneur the world welcomed her and told her how wonderful she was? Of course not.

Who was Madam C. J. Walker? Well, she was America's first black female millionaire, and the first woman of any race to become a self-made millionaire. She built an empire from virtually nothing in one of the most spectacular rags-to-riches stories in U.S. history. Madam C. J. Walker's dream started becoming a reality when one day, washing her hair, she noticed that it all started to fall out. So, there in the midst of personal tragedy, she changed the world by providing hair products for African Americans, creating job opportunities and developing and pioneering a unique system of multilevel marketing.

By the time she died at the age of fifty one she was revered as a philanthropist who donated to scholarship funds, helped the NAACP and campaigned to end lynching. Madam C. J. Walker helped to build a black YMCA in Indianapolis and restored Frederick Douglass's home in Washington. She had a vision, a goal, and the ability to stick with her vision regardless of the hardships she encountered.

My Objectives

At this stage, my main objective is to remind and inform you of the fact that part of being a success comes from learning from the struggles you have in your lives, understanding how others who struggled before us can help to avoid making the same mistakes and then being able to appreciate the journey during your creative process.

What do these three people previously mentioned have in common? People may have thought they were different but very few believed or saw them as visionaries or creatives, especially earlier in their careers. Now, all three of them are seen as extraordinary people. Extraordinary because regardless of their struggles, they remained steadfast in accomplishing their goals, irrespective of the situations they encountered.

And I am here to tell you now that you, yes you, have the ability to create your own mini or maybe gigantic empire right where you are.

But you have to believe, you have to get started, and you have to persevere through thick and thin, regardless of what situations you meet.

When you are trying to reach your goals, there will be obstacles along the way; there is no doubt about that. However, if you can see those obstacles for what they are - goal posts to test your grit - you will realise how much you want that goal or dream. Please trust me and believe me that nothing worthwhile was created in a day and nothing worthwhile that you really value is just given to you. It is really only when you work for what you want that you realize the value in what you get.

I hope this book will aid and help you in taking the necessary steps to help you start dreaming again if you have stopped dreaming. Or to start dreaming. Period!

Start dreaming by working towards your goals one step at a time. But please be aware that it is impossible to get there if you do not know where you are going. And trust me, all it takes is one baby step to get started and then momentum will thrust you forward to heights you have never imagined. But you need to have a plan; a plan that will give you directions to a better life for both you and your family. If you don't have a family, planning will help you better yourself in ways you never thought possible. The main requirements are a vision and a plan.

Who is this book for? Who will it help?

This book is for you, the dreamer or the person who wants to dream but is unsure how to get started. This book is for you, the mother who wants to teach her children the value of believing in themselves and working towards a goal from a very young age. This book is for you, the father who wants to improve himself and then in turn help his family succeed, while in the process leaving a blueprint for his children and others to follow. This book is for the children who really don't know where or how to begin developing or trying to fulfil their dreams.

But most of all, this book is for you, for you and your personal circumstances, for you and the trials and tribulations you face every day. For you, the one person who needs to believe that there are more treasures locked up inside of them that they just need to get out.

Or as Steve Jobs so elegantly stated, during his version of Apple's ground-breaking 'Think Different' video, "Here's to the crazy ones. The misfits. The rebels. The troublemakers. The round pegs in the square holes. The ones who see things differently. They're not fond of rules. And they have no respect for the status quo. You can quote them, disagree with them, glorify or vilify them. About the only thing, you can't do is ignore them. Because they change things. They push the human race forward. And while some may see them as the crazy ones, we see genius. Because the people who are crazy enough to think they can change the world are the ones who do.
- Rob Siltanen

So, grab a pen or pencil and a journal to record your thoughts and come with me and let's start changing the world. Because I truly believe that by starting with you, we can change your world, and through changing your world we can make a bigger impact on the universe. And when we start making a positive impact on the universe, other people's lives change, which will impact more lives, and so the process will continue.

The Start of Hope

Ever since I can remember I have been going to church with my mother. One of the things church did for me was to give me hope. It still does. It also gave me a sense of dignity, that as a young man maybe I had a a place in this world. And what is a person without hope?

I trust that everyone believes or wants to believe in something, whether it is a spirit or their own personal God, whatever form or fashion. Personally, throughout the writing of this book, I know that there is a higher power guiding and directing my steps.

I feel as though I am blessed daily and I truly believe that everyone has access to their own blessings. However, the one key factor I believe when thinking about my blessing is that I have to look for the blessing each day. Something as simple as having the opportunity to open the door for someone, or as simple as saying yes ma'am and no ma'am. Even the opportunity and ability to be able to get out of my bed in the morning is a true blessing. What have you been taking for granted that you should feel blessed about? I tell you, you will be surprised how many blessings will appear right before your eyes if you really look.

Open your mind's eye and don't merely look at what's happening in front of you but see what's happening right in front of you, and then realize that you need to enjoy the moment because it is the only moment you can experience.

Recently I was out for my walk, usually a distance of three to four miles. I had my headphones on and I was in a zone. It was around 6 am, slightly raining and dark. As I was walking, I noticed just one person in that whole ninety minutes; a single car drove past. People weren't up and about yet, they normally would have been but it was Christmas Eve.

After walking about a mile and a half, zoned out and in my own world, I trod on a piece of paper and all of a sudden it shocked me back to reality. I was literally in a zone and couldn't really tell you what was going on around me. I think we are like this in life. We are so used to doing the same things daily, having the same routine that we don't pay attention to what is happening right in front of us. So, my message to you and myself is to pay attention to your life.

Don't just drift through life, moment to moment, hour to hour, and day to day, without paying attention to your life. Because by paying attention, you will see those blessings which are right in front of you and, even more importantly, you will have the opportunity to be a blessing to someone else. Then you will see the goodness that life has for you, and then you can see the reasons why you need to be thankful.

As I sit and write this book, there is no way I feel that I could just sit down as I do and have paragraphs and paragraphs just flow through me without some power working through me. This is why I truly believe that there is a power that sustains the universe all the way down to little old me. However, in order for us to get the best out of ourselves, we need to be aware of our existence each day, mindful of our feeling and the environment we are in. Aware of the opportunities we have to see life for what it should be; happiness and a celebration, not just a daily struggle.

However, may I point out here that I believe that all of us have the option to believe what we truly want to believe. So, whatever you believe in, I truly hope that it gives you power, wisdom, and love, but most of all, I truly wish that you receive hope. Hope that will inspire you to live a fuller and more adventurous life than you ever thought possible.

Human Beings

I believe that we, as human beings, have an innate ability to not only want to succeed, but also to go out and find what it is that make us successful. As human beings, we are uniquely adept at creating and utilizing systems to help us become and stay successful. Look at all the businesses that surround us, look at the railways, the airplanes, the stores, even the clothes we wear. Understand that every single thing you see once only existed in someone else's imagination.

So, I believe that if you can see and believe it in your mind's eye, work hard for it, then you can conceive and manifest anything you desire. But you really need to want it, have a deep desire, and have a game plan and work hard to get what your heart desires. However, you have to be both a realist and understand your limitations. What do I mean? Well, if I am 5ft 2ins, with little or no basketball skills, and want to play in the NBA there's a good chance that it is not going to happen.

Look, I have been on both sides of the track, one side where I hated just about everything about my life and didn't think that I had any major purpose in life, drifting from day to day with no ambitions and no dreams.

And I have also been on the other side, where I am now, where I feel that each day is a gift and I can tell you this side is more pleasant. I find myself more proactive, but most of all I find that I just love the feeling of being able to help others have more productive and meaningful lives. But it is not easy to be happy each day. You have to work at it because your mind is an incredible muscle, it will look for issues and troubles for you to deal with. However, I really believe that there is a divine power, and if as human beings we include it in our journey, the path would be much smoother and our minds a lot calmer. OK, let's get something straight; each day you will have negative thoughts that come to you, but it really depends on you and how you choose to deal with them. You can use your negative thoughts as fuel for greatness, or you can listen to them and accept what your mind is telling you or use the negative thoughts to soak up the darkness. It is entirely up to you. But I will tell you this; your life can be amazing if you really want it to be, starting with one thought at a time. So, please come on, get aboard and let's start living a much happier life.

What do you hope you will get out of this reading?

I believe that the human species is an amazing creature and I also believe each one of us can do well and leave a legacy that can live on long after we have left this planet. Qualities such as optimism and attitude allow us as humans to chart our own course in life, to pick ourselves up when a tragedy has knocked us and then to excel while using that event's lesson of life to help us improve ourselves. In a single word, to me, the greatest vision we can have is based on HOPE, an optimistic attitude that is based on an expectation of positive outcomes related to events and circumstances in one's life.

I truly hope that this book not only provides you with some sort of direction in your life, but, most importantly that you get the understanding that life is about steps. Nothing is ever done in one big swoop, or at least nothing that will stand the test of time, which really means anything to anyone. Things that have real value to us as human beings are things that we work hard for ourselves. When you have put in blood, sweat, and tears over time into any project, these are the things that really matter. These are the things you remember and remember for a lifetime.

If you think about getting to your destination in the mornings, you don't suddenly get up and within two minutes appear in your place of employment unless, of course, you work from home.

Now there are logical steps which you have to take to accomplish your goals and get to your destination. For instance, the first step starts with you waking up in the morning. The next step is that you go to the bathroom, then have a shower, get dressed, have breakfast, pack your lunch, then get in your car, and finally drive to work. Everything has a process. Your life and goals are no different. Everything has a process, and the sooner we understand the process, the simpler our lives will be.

If you think of a woman having a baby, that baby does not suddenly appear because the woman is pregnant. Once the woman is pregnant, there is a timeframe and process involved before that baby makes his or her grand entrance into the world. Again, it is the same thought process in terms of getting your goals accomplished.

First of all, you have to know what you want (the women/parents want to have a baby). Then there is a time frame and preparation process to make for the child to be born (in terms of your goals you have to write down what you want and lay out a plan of how you are going to get what you want). And finally, when the baby arrives (your goals are accomplished). It is a lifetime that you have to take care of your child (it is the same for your goals). Once you accomplish your goals, it is a continual process of redeveloping and rethinking how you are going to remain successful.

Getting up in the morning

This book is designed to help you accomplish your life's goals through having a look at events in my life that I hope you can relate to. Each chapter starts off with a few positive words or quotes followed by a story based on an event that happened to me. After the story, we talk about the lesson I learned from that particular story. Once you have finished these sections, we have a group of questions which will get you to thinking about and reflecting on how the story can help you in your life.

Good luck on your journey and may the winds blow on the back of your neck and propel you towards a glorious future.

Chapter One

MOTIVATION

"Be wise in the way you act towards outsiders; make the most of every opportunity. Let your conversations be always full of grace, seasoned with salt, so that you may know how to answer everyone."

—Colossians 4:5-6

[MW1]

MOTIVATION

Once upon a time, there was a little boy who like most little boys his age had no hopes or dreams he could think of. Each day was like the last, and when night came, it just brought upon more nothingness for him. He loved his family, but so desperately wanted to have a meaning for his life.

His mother, father, and grandparents, along with his siblings, poured into his life with encouragement the best way they could, but even with no hopes or dreams for himself, he knew - he just knew he wanted his life to be extraordinary. Even if he didn't know what the word extraordinary fully meant. But he had this feeling that he was brought here on this planet for a special reason.

I wrote those paragraphs when I was ten years old. It reminds me now of so many students I see today living their lives with little or no hopes and dreams. My single greatest hope for my life is that through my interactions with these students, I can offer them some encouragement and be a role model for them. You see, it wasn't that long ago that I felt the same way and some men and women took the time to pour into my life, helping me to develop an understanding of who I was and the routes which were available to me.

In my classroom I often tell my students stories of my life, in the hope that they will realize that I too, am a human, and that I bleed for goodness and rightness for my soul and the world just like they do. We just use different phrases to express ourselves. I hope that through my interactions, our souls will intertwine even if it is for the shortest of periods and at the end we can made a difference in each other's journey.

Life is about taking the ordinary and making it extraordinary, taking chances and making constructive decisions, some of them calculated and others on the spur of the moment.

So, with your gifts attached to your ordinary dreams, you could end up having an extraordinary life experience. While helping others to accomplish their goals, please remember this; by helping others achieve their goals, you also help yourself accomplish your own. But understand this also, try never to do a good deal wanting something in return. Just be grateful and full of gratitude that you were able to have an impact on someone else's life. You will never know if those simple words or gestures may spur that person to go on and change the world in their own way. I feel it's our duty to help impact the world in a positive way.

The stories which will follow are my memories of a series of events which occurred in my life, and have brought me to a wonderful place in my life. I have discovered that I am responsible for my life and no one else is. During that journey, there have been many times when I had to get up from both tragedy and heartache. Nonetheless, I made it, and so can you.

"Too blessed to be stressed," as my mother, Mrs. Pernell Lawrence, would say. Too blessed to be stressed. One thing that Pernell always insisted on was that all of her kids had dreams and goals.

But she also made sure that we knew that those dreams and goals were not enough to have, you need to have a motive and place actions behind those dreams and goals. When we didn't feel like going to school, that motivation pushed us toward our goals, in this case just getting to the spot, our classroom. Not only did she say this to us verbally, but she also demonstrated it every day with her actions, and sometimes actions speak louder than words, especially to impressionable children. Actions such as taking on more than one job to help ensure that her children had food to eat and clothes to wear. Actions which demonstrated to all of her children that it is up to you to get it done, whatever it is. In other words, if it's going to be, she would say, then it has to be up to me.

MY ENTRANCE TO THE WORLD

My journey began in a hospital in Orangeburg, South Carolina. The doctors told my mother, "Mrs. Lawrence, it doesn't look good and we need to operate on your baby. However, once we open him up, if we don't find what we are looking for, we will close him up; send him home with you with our prayers. In other words, Mrs. Lawrence, from our past experiences of this type of situation, we don't expect him to live more than 6 weeks. We are so sorry." However, those six weeks have turned into decades and it has turned out amazingly well for me. Amazingly well.

What a wonderful awaking I have had during my life journey so far. I hope that you, too, will be awakened by the stories and lessons in this book and begin living your blessed life as it was meant to be lived. Enjoyable!

Blessed and highly favoured because, believe me, you are truly blessed and highly favoured. How, first of all you were born? You just have to believe it, start walking in your blessed path and start acting like it.

Make your life both your magnificent obsession and an amazing adventure. Good luck on your magnificent adventure.

"Try to be a rainbow in someone's cloud."
—**Maya Angelou**

LESSON LEARNED

The stories that we tell others are the lifeblood of our souls and our society. It is essential that in some way all of us tell our stories in some form or fashion. For our stories could be the fuel that helps someone else solve a problem, or easily be the catalyst to a more meaningful life for someone we may never ever meet. But you will never know if your story is never told to the world. It is your choice and one that could impact the world in ways you could never imagine.

Reflection Questions

Think about these questions, then
write your responses in a journal or notebook.

1. What motivates you to achieve your goals and dreams to help you accomplish them? List them, being specific in your description of the motivation.

2. Do you have a plan to achieve your goals? Be specific and intentional about how you will accomplish each goal. Develop a map for your journey toward each goal.

3. Have you developed a list of items that will have to wait until you have achieved specific goals?

4. If you don't meet your goals, who would be disappointed or feel let down? To whom do your goals matter besides you? In other words, "What is your WHY?"

"The longer I live, the more I understand that the quality of my life depends on both the quality of my relations and my why."
—Renaldo Lawrence

Chapter Two

FOLLOW YOUR OWN PATH

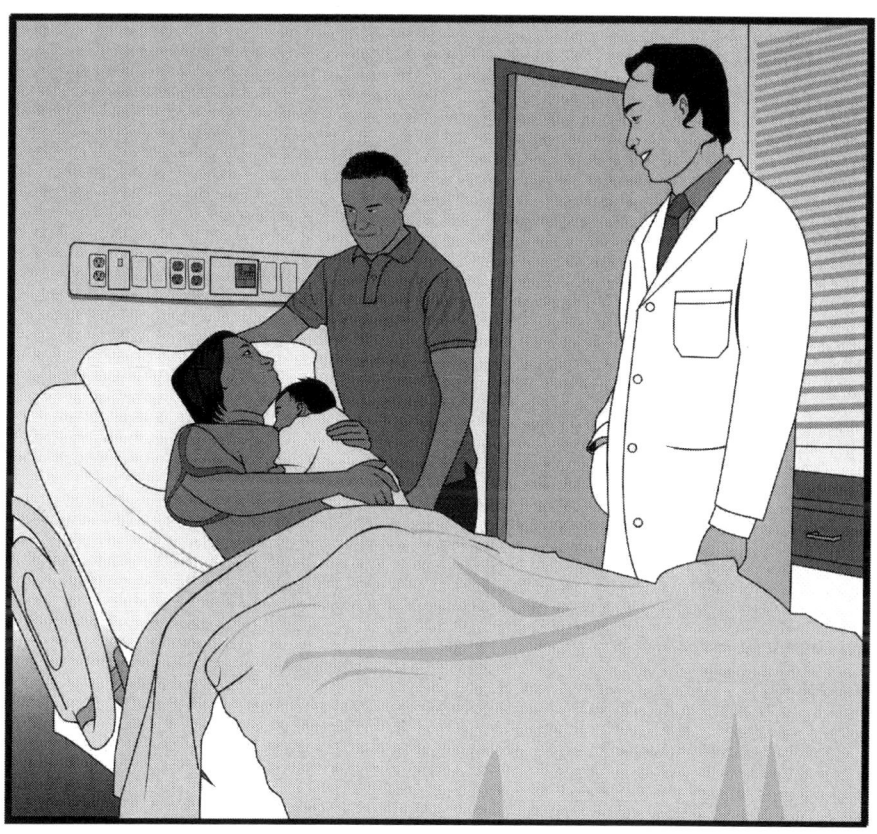

"The longer I live the more I understand that the quality of my life depends on both the quality of my relations and my why." -

—Renaldo Lawrence

On the morning of March 30th, 1957 in the Orangeburg, South Carolina hospital, both of my parents felt helpless, Pernell, my mother, giving birth after the doctor told her that there were complications and Andrew Lawrence, my father sitting worried and waiting.

It was a bright sunny day. The sun was shining extremely bright for this time of the year and as my mother tells me, "You could hear the wind howl outside the hospital windows." Inside the hospital, it was a pleasant temperature, the atmosphere was calm (but this was about to change as far as my parents were concerned) as nurses and doctors went about their jobs attending to patients. As my mother continued telling me the story, she remembers feeling very apprehensive, and she had the feeling deep in her soul that something wasn't exactly right. Then....

"Oh, my God, my baby is here!" Pernell said.

The doctor had yet to break the news to my mother. As she quieted, he informed her, "Pernell, your baby is... not complete."

He continued, and my parents were trying hard to understand. "His insides are twisted and not connected as a normal child's organs are. We are sorry to say that based on our past experiences we really don't think he has more than six weeks to live. We are so sorry, but only six weeks. We will try everything that we can in our powers to help him, but we needed to make sure you understand what is going on."

After three days in the hospital and many tests, the head nurse visited my parents. "Mrs. Lawrence, we have run the tests and again come to the same conclusion. Your son has about six weeks to live, we are so sorry. His insides are twisted, and his cords are not linked properly. We have done all we can."

As my mom tells the story now, she says to me that as the doctor's words finished coming out of his mouth, God dropped a thought into her heart. "God had another plan for the baby's life. This is not the end." To this day, I have always felt that God had a special plan for my life, a plan for me to serve, and, like my mother, to help whoever it was possible to help.

Some years later, my mother ran into the same head nurse who looked after me in the hospital. Mom remembers their conversation like this: "I am so sorry, Mrs. Lawrence, I know that your son died. I want you to know that we did as much as we could for him." My mother replied, "Actually he is alive, 21 years old and playing basketball." I can only imagine how shocked the nurse was. You see, man dreams and makes plans but only God knows what your life will turn out to be.

My mother, Pernell, was also born under challenging circumstances and she survived and prospered. Pernell survived because she developed a *why* and I think that if anyone of us is going to be successful, then we need to develop our own *why*. It is that *why*, that you have to attach yourself to, and it is, that *why* which will help you propel yourself to greatness.

We all come into this world and are presented with different challenges that must be overcome. There is no single right path which will lead us all to wisdom or prosperity. We each have choices to make and eventually, we must make those choices based on our past experiences.

Just the thought of my hospital story takes me back to the story my grandmother told me about my mom being born before she, my grandmother lost a set of twins. Elders in the community told my grandmother that before your next child is born, name the child after the earth and the child would live. Well, that's what my grandmother did. The name 'Pernell' means 'little rock' or 'of the earth'. How strange that years later, Pernell's nickname was 'Mud'.

As stated in Ecclesiastes 4:9-12, "Two are better than one, because they have a good reward for their toil. For if they fall, one will lift up his fellow. But woe to him who is alone when he falls and has not another to lift him up! Again, if two lie together, they keep warm, but how can one keep warm alone? And though a man might prevail against one who is alone, two will withstand him - a threefold chord is not quickly broken." Well, that child was my mother, and like so many others in our community I am eternally grateful, and I thank God every day that she lives.

Life is an amazing adventure and remarkably different for each of us. This is the reason I believe that it is impossible for anyone to give us a roadmap. No one's journey is ever the same. However, we all have common experiences which can be shared and are fundamental in maintaining close bonds between us. As we share our stories we lighten our loads and overcome adversity. As the saying goes, a burden shared is a burden halved.

In my experience, most people feel that they need to navigate through this journey of life all by themselves, but time and time again I have found that trying to get through this adventure called Life is easier when I share the experience with others.

WHAT ARE YOUR GOALS?

I have encountered so many people who are already living their dreams. Some artists started with little or nothing, not even able to afford the paint required to complete their paintings. However, they found a way through thick and thin to make it happen. This is the key to life, I think.

Regardless of the circumstances, you have to attack the problem as hard as you can, then find a solution and, in order to benefit others, share your newly acquired wisdom. It is called the circle of life. No excuses.

For example, some people would love to complete their education by acquiring a Masters or Ph.D. but have no idea if they can make it. Yet in spite of their busy home lives, they found a way to attend school or complete a home study course. My mother taught me this lesson years ago. My mother didn't want her six children to ever complain about going to school so at the age of 43, she went back to school to earn her high school diploma. A priceless example of what hard work, being a role model, and having a dream can do for anyone. However, she didn't do it alone. She had the support of her family for the easy courses and the tough ones. Her motivation was clear and compelling. Not completing the degree was never part of the equation.

Motivation + goals + dreams + support = meeting your goal! However, to me it was a statement that said, anything you want to do it is possible, but you have to seriously want it to happen, and then put in the hard work to make it happen.

I'm here to tell you that in my observational experience, if you really want to make it, there is a way. I've seen it on the farm when I was growing up. I've seen it in my community where I grew up. I have seen it in schools that refused to give up on their students. In each of these situations, the individuals found a way to succeed, through hard work and perseverance along with motivation for accomplishing those dreams and missions.

But, you must be prepared to push, persevere, and fight, even more. Are you ready? It is a question that only you can answer.

DISCERNING YOUR GIFTS

The first step in the process is to find your gifts. Your gifts are what will propel you toward a happier life. By working with your gifts and believing in your goal(s), you can accomplish it, and help change the world in the process. I truly believe that one of the only ways to be happy during your life is to do what you are happy doing and that is what makes your heart sing.

One of the gifts I was blessed with is the ability to play basketball. However, although I was blessed with this gift, it took me years and years to get to a point where that gift started to be a blessing for me. Not only did it take me years, but the right people also had to come into my life at the right time. And I needed to recognise that the opportunity that lay before me was one that I wanted to pursue.

The gift of being able to play basketball to a high level gave me the chance to make a lot of people happy when they attended the games. It also gave me the opportunity to attend Appalachian State University on a scholarship, where not only did we win two championships but I also met some people who have remained friends to me till this day; dear friends.

From Appalachian State University I went on to be drafted by the Los Angeles Clippers, and although I got cut, it was my gift that allowed me to be exposed to that level of excellence. My gift didn't stop there. I have played in countries such as France, Sweden, England, Argentina, and South America. In England, I was fortunate enough to score 73 points in a game; that earned me a place in the Guinness Books of Records. I also hold many of the scoring records in the British basketball league and ended up being the fourth highest scorer in the history of British basketball; all through working my gift. And the best part of my gift? I have a family who are happy, blessed, each of them working their own gifts. They came from?....you got it right, me working my gifts. By playing basketball in England, I was able to meet my wife, Janis and as they say, the rest is history. A blessed history.

As a matter of fact, my son, Andrew, played in the 2012 Olympics for the Great Britain basketball team. Andrew is now working his gift at the time of writing, playing basketball in Paris. I am also blessed to have a daughter, Jessica, who is an English Literature major and is also working in her gifts as a social media manager for one of the largest magazines in London. But neither would have would have been born or discovered their gifts unless I understood, developed, and lived in my gift. That's how important it is to find, nurture, and live in your gifts.

It was years later, having played in South America, Argentina, Sweden, Finland, and England, that I realized that the gift of basketball was really a gift to help propel me into the career I am in now; helping people, a teacher, author, parent, husband, and God-fearing man. But I will tell you that I believe that in my life and yours there are gifts stored up inside of you that you just need to find and use. There is no way that I ever would have thought that the skills I learned from playing basketball, speaking before audiences, performing in front of thousands of people playing basketball, getting my Masters, would ever lead me to where I am now. Ever!

But let me make something clear here, I spent hours and hours and hours on those courts developing those skills. I played in the mornings before school, at lunchtime, after school, at night time, on weekends and after church. It was my magnificent obsession for years.

One thing that I always remembered growing up, however, was that I never wanted to be anyone else. I just wanted to be me, but I wanted to develop some of the amazing basketball skills and character attributes that people like Julius Erving, Dr. J, exhibited during their careers. So, I believe that, as with me, you should not want to be anyone else but the amazing person you are. You should look at others you might admire, try to develop some of the character attributes they possess, tie them to your gift and make your life the best life you possibly can for you and your family.

What I have come to understand is that sometimes your gifts and blessings are being used and enhanced because you are being set up for bigger and better things. The gifts you are developing now could be the gifts you need to help the world in another capacity. Let me use my life as an example and explain what I mean.

I know now that the basketball gift was just a set-up to give me the opportunity to help teachers and educators around the world help their students succeed. Through companies such as Adobe, Apple, Microsoft, lynda.com, and LinkedIn Learning I have been able to teach on a worldwide stage. Some of my work can be found at: www.lynda.com/renaldolawrence

You see, when I was traveling to all those countries, I was looking at their school systems (I have a Physical Education degree from Appalachian State University), noticing how students and teachers from different parts of the world were communicating with each other. Little did I know that all that knowledge would be as valuable to me as it is now.

But it was basketball that gave me the opportunity to travel and learn. I am now one of the top educational e-Learning authors in the world. I couldn't have thought that bouncing a little ball would give me the opportunity to help change the world, especially one who didn't care that much for school.

One major point I need to make sure you understand is that just because you have a gift, that doesn't mean that the gift will be one that will help propel you towards your life goals. After identifying the goal, this is where the work really begins. And I mean Really Begins.

Once you find your gift(s), you have to learn how to incorporate them into your life, your family's lives, and your livelihood, then you will never work another day in your life. Believe me that not only will your gifts make room for you, but they will also allow you to make rooms for others. And when you have others working together with you, there is nothing you can't accomplish.

As written in Matthew 18:19-20, "Again I say to you that if two of you agree on earth concerning anything that they ask, it will be done for them by My Father in heaven. For where two or three are gathered together in my name, I am there in the midst of them."

Stop reading for a moment and think to yourself now. What is it that I love to do and would do even if I wasn't paid to do it? One thing to remember is this, "Sometimes you have to do what you have to do now, just to get where you really want to be in the future." As written in Zechariah 4:10, "Do not despise these small beginnings." You have to just get started and getting started can be just as simple as writing your goals on a piece of paper. So that you can see your vision every day. This should be your daily roadmap to a better life.

So now let's get started by thinking and writing down our goals.

YOUR TASK:

Please take out paper and pencil, before you start writing, think about what you really want in your life, then consider your gifts if you know what they are. If you don't know your gifts right now, that's fine. When you start writing, just make a list of everything you want in your life. Don't worry now, just write. However, if you know your gifts, then ask yourself the following questions.

How can your gifts help you accomplish your desired goals? As my mother, Pernell, always said to us growing up, "Where there is a will, there is always a way." And part of your life's mission is to find that way. When you have your list or recognize your gift, would you like a fabulous shortcut to the process? I thought you would!

One shortcut to the process is to find someone who has done what you want to do and has the time and inclination to speak with you. Ask how they got where they are. You can gain a significant quantity of information this way and possibly cut down on the time it may take you to reach your goal(s). However, you must prepare yourself for this encounter since your source may have limited time. Think through the process, write your questions down and practice asking the questions. You will be surprised how much people will want to help you.

I have never found anyone in any authority who doesn't want to talk about themselves and the path they took to be successful. Remember, when you meet them, it is all about them and their experiences, and not necessarily what they can do for you. I have had to learn that sometimes you just need to shut up, listen, and think deeply about the conversation you are having. If you are too engaged with trying to get something, you just might miss the bits of wisdom that could take you to the next level. You want to ensure that you look and act professionally. Do your research in terms of finding out what the person likes. What are their charities? What did they do as a young person growing up to help propel them to the position they are in today? All this will give you conversation, and the best part of the discussion is that if you have done your homework, the person will be impressed. But remember, it is not about you at this stage of the game. You just require information to help you accomplish your goals.

Recall what I said earlier, who doesn't want to tell you how they made it? This career expert may want to become your mentor in the future. Be prepared to get the most out of the experience. In the reflective questions, there are just a few questions to help you get started. However, if you do your research, you just might find the answers yourself. Trust me; there is nothing like a person who has done their research, found out what the issues or problems are, and can come up with a solution. Nothing is impossible if you are prepared to work and find a solution to your problems!

When you are searching for what makes your heart sing, it is imperative that you have a strong mindset. Once you set your heart on a goal, write it down. Then, review your goal daily, taking one step toward it each day. The key to the process is getting started with a concrete action.

It is so important that you have a focused, die-hard attitude. You will certainly run into people with negative attitudes who will tell you that it can't be done, you can't meet your goals. Even crazier, if you are not careful, you may talk yourself out of it. This is why it is so important that you do at least one thing a day as you follow your path to your goal. Keep track of your progress along the way so that you can continually measure your success. By doing this, it will help you to check your progress continually and with each success you can start and continue to encourage yourself.

Trust me, having a positive mindset and a die-hard attitude will come in handy during times when you might not see any progress. That's why it is so important to commit your goals to writing so that you can see and remember where you are going. Completing at least one task based on accomplishing your goals every day and making note of it helps you visualize and see just how far you've come and how committed you are in pursuing your goals.

If your progress is not measurable, your goal may not be attainable. Monitoring your progress can help you monitor your commitment and make it real!

As a friend said to me the other day, "If I was going to Scotland, do you think I would start with a map or just start walking with no sense of direction?" The rational answer is that you would find a map. So, if you would find a map to travel to Scotland or anywhere in the world, then why would you leave your life to chance? Doesn't it make sense to create a map to help direct you through your life?

"The world needs people who can change it for the better." If your goals involve helping other people and making their lives better, then you are on your way to making society better and accomplishing your goals. And there is no better feeling than knowing you have helped improve someone else's life, even if it is nothing but a smile and a map.

LESSON LEARNED

"Remember, life is all about your perspective." All that seems negative is not negative, especially if you use the experience to learn something new. When I have a negative experience or hear bad news about a project, I gain leverage by finding an alternative approach. I lived, in spite of what the doctors said, not just to play basketball at twenty-one, but to grow much older, write this book, and to help change the world! Ready to come on board with me? Your life will never be the same again.

You have two choices in any situation, you can react or you can respond. What do I mean? In any situation, you have the choice of just reacting to a situation based primarily on your feelings. Never a smart or great idea. Or you can respond. Responding means you have thought about the situation and made a conscious decision based on all the facts available.

Just remember too, that it is equally important to transform the person you see in the mirror on the outside, as it is to transform that person on the inside.

Reflection Questions

1. Are you currently experiencing roadblocks to accomplishing goals? Be aware that a change of perspective could remove those roadblocks and allow you to move more quickly toward your goals?

    If so, write down the goal and the roadblock. Then, develop an alternative approach by taking a new perspective through which you can view the roadblock.

    You may have to talk with supporters and friends to help you discover a new way of approaching the problem, but trust me it will be worth it.

    Write down the new approach and the new options, or the leverage you gain by adopting a new point of view. You will not be sorry that you did.

2. Have you written your goals down? Can you find someone who has already accomplished what you are trying to achieve? This can be even from afar. For instance, I have a few people who are my mentors, and I have never met them in my life. Tony Robbins, Eric Thomas, Gary Vaynerchuk, Julius Erving (I have met Julius), T.D. Jakes, and Joel Osteen. I use what they say on social media as a way of helping keep in contact with my goals and dreams every day.

3. Ok, now that you have written down your goals, have you written at least one thing that can help you accomplish them today? If you have not, then do so now. If you have, then get started making a start toward accomplishing your goals. One step or task at a time, but you have to get started. Oh yeah, don't forget the life map.

Chapter Three

THE POWER
OF I AM

*In Matthew 12:37 it states that, "For by your words you will be
justified, and by your words you will be condemned."*

Spending time at Bosie Caldwell's (my grandfather) house was always a positive experience for me. Even when I didn't want to get up at 6 am, there was always excitement just thinking about what the day held for us. There was never a dull moment because if I wasn't doing chores, I was riding horses, hunting, climbing trees, feeding animals, picking fruit from the trees, walking the dog, picking corn, watching TV or just hanging out with my older brother Marshall.

I have many positive memories of spending time on the farm, but there is one thing that I always remembered about my grandfather. He was always particular when choosing words to speak about himself. I always paid attention to both my grandfather and father because as a young boy, these men were my measuring sticks to what I would become as a man.

It is always tough to become something if you have never seen it or have no way of measuring it. For example, if I wanted to become a lawyer, then I know I would need to take courses and go to law school, Otherwise, it would be impossible for me to become a lawyer. Likewise, if I wanted to become a farmer, it would take me a while to understand how to cultivate the land properly, feed the animals, and understand the cycles of the weather and so on. So, I figured if I wanted to be a man who had strong values and a sense of what it took to take care for and love a family, it only made sense that I observed those men to see how they handled themselves and the things they did daily so that I could hopefully learn. To learn what to do in different situations and, just as importantly, what not to do in others.

When my grandfather used to tell me stories during the days and at the end of each day, he would tell me how important two words were. Funny because I didn't think much of them growing up but, like his teachings, these two words have taken on tremendous meaning to me as an adult. Time is amazing. It seems that the longer I am on this planet, the more I appreciate the lessons taught to me in my youth. My grandfather, Bosie Caldwell's most important words were, "I AM." The term I AM, was used all the time and I can tell you honestly that I don't ever remember a negative word coming from Bosie Caldwell's mouth after the term I AM. Bosie was a confident man, confident in himself and the path he was on and he took it as his personal goal, I believe now, to ensure that I was a positive soul.

I remember a particular incident where my grandfather had a conversation with my mother about finding the money to buy a washing machine that my grandmother needed. Well, everyone was kind of upset because at that particular time the amount of money required was not available. Now you have to understand that my grandfather owned thousands of acres of land, so money wasn't a problem. He just couldn't access the money quickly. I will never forget the words he spoke during the family meeting. He said to us, "All of you listen to me, I am Bosie Caldwell and all my life I have built a reputation that is respectable and honored by men of all different colors and creed. I will get the money and we will purchase the washing machine, Buck." (Buck was the nickname my grandfather used to call my grandmother.) I don't know how he did it but the next week we had that washing machine in the house. It was a powerful moment for me, especially if you understand the times of racial disharmony during the late 60s. This was a powerful symbol to see as a young black boy. Powerful!

A week later, my grandfather and I were sitting on the porch. This was always one of my favorite moments because of the amazing stories he told me about himself and his life. The sun was going down, it was a quiet night on the farm, all the animals were settling in and from where we were sitting, we could see the other families in the community preparing for the night. I often sat on the porch with my grandfather during the evening, and I took these times as learning times, although at that age that wasn't the term I would use. But man did I learn a lot and today more than ever I treasure those memories.

During our conversation, Bosie Caldwell imparted some knowledge to me that would forever have an impact on the way I think, how I handled myself, dealt with other people and even now, how I would help raise my children.

He said to me, "Boy," he always used to call me boy, funny for a period of time I thought that was my name. He continued "Do you know why I am powerful and can get whatever I need for my family?" "No sir," I replied. "Well, I am going to tell you. In this life, I have learned that the only real thing a man has is his word, and if he doesn't honor his word, then regardless of how much money he has he is not worth a grain of salt. I am who I am today because I keep my word and treat people like I want to be treated."

It would take some years for that lesson to sink in, but until this day, there is never a day that goes by that I don't live that lesson I learned on that quiet, peaceful evening, just my grandfather and me. A man who knew who he was trying to help a young boy become who he needed to be.

I was soon to see for most people; this was not the case when I ventured out into the world. One incident comes to mind to illustrate how impact the words I AM can have or how it can take on so many meanings depending on the individual or situation.

I remember during a class I was in during high school, a teacher said, "I am so sick of how this class acts and I am tired of it." The funny thing is that I remember so well how uninteresting those teacher's classes were.

So, I have heard the term, I AM in so many situations, but the message I want to share with you is that your I AMs are so important. Be careful of how you use the term and whenever you do use it, make sure there is something positive coming behind those words. I AM can literally change how you feel about yourself and influence your world as you see it.

My grandfather's lesson was a potent one for me that evening, even as a boy. What a stark contrast in terms of the use of the words. I AM. That experience has always stuck with me. No, I am not overwhelmed with happiness all the time; however, when it comes to how I feel about myself, there has never been a negative I AM coming out of my mouth about me. Those feelings come from my grandfather's influence, and man do I thank him.

Was my grandfather a cocky man? Am I? No, not in the slightest. The world tells people on a consistent basis who they are and who they are not and now with social media, it seems that life and death are determined by how many likes and follows we have. I refuse to accept what the world says about me. I just refuse! Of course, I get things wrong and take full responsibility for my mistakes and missteps on my job or in my daily life, for any of the challenging situations I may land in. Nevertheless, I must apply an alternative perspective here. I am nobody's situation and neither should you be. Ever! So, when you ever use these words I AM, you make sure that you are using them for good towards you and not against you. Thus, the good news I wanted to share with you today is that you can choose the words that come after I AM. Make your words powerful and make sure they reflect the powerful human being you are because you are blessed and magnificent. You just have to believe it.

REFORMING YOUR TALK SO YOU CAN DIRECT YOUR WALK

I am a very observant person and pay close attention to people and how they act, but most importantly how they speak and the words that come out of their mouth. If you really want to know someone, start listening consistently to the language they are using about themselves, or even more importantly, listen to how they speak to people who may not have as much as they do. Stay silent and within 10 minutes you can just about sum up any individual.

As an exercise, the next time you are listening to some of your friends or even to yourself when you are having a discussion, pay attention to how many time you hear phrases like, I am tired, I am so stressed, I am so unhappy, and even I am so not worthy. Saying those terms regardless of the situation does you no good and will continually give you a negative mentality whether you realize it or not.

Sometimes you have to start calling things as you wish them to be, not as they are. And sometimes you have to go out on a limb and say these positive terms even if you don't feel like it. It is your life, and it is essential that you live the best life you can. If you are against yourself, then you don't have any real hope of making it and being successful. Learn to live in and work out of your principles and not your feelings. Please remember that you have all manner of potential deep inside you, don't be one of those people who never reach their potential by not trying to live your dreams and accomplishing your goals. You have

24 glorious hours in your day; what you think about and do is entirely up to you. Please make them count for something.

Remember that the world is looking at you and determining how to treat you by the way you treat yourself. So why not try replacing those negative terms with terms such as I am happy, I am blessed, I am wonderful, I am so powerful, I am magnificent, I am healthy, and I am so gifted and talented. Remember to call things as you wish them to be. Sometimes it will be a stretch, but what other choice do you have? Talk negatively about yourself? I don't think so.

So, it is vital that you try hard to keep a positive mindset, keep on praising yourself and understanding that if you don't praise yourself, there might not be a chance for you to consume any positivity during that day. On the other hand, I also realize how detrimental those negative I AMs can be and how they can have such a negative impact on your daily life. So, stay positive and make your I AMs work for you. When you get up in the morning, arm yourself by listening to something positive on the way to work. Make sure you listen or read before you get to work, this is the key. Put on your "**Armour**" for the battles you will have to face during the day, and by arming yourself for battle, you will be able to deal with issues with a different outlook. Then when you enter that environment, you will be the light and you can shine. Easy? No, not always, but if you want a positive life, you sometimes need to be the positive light in a dark environment.

LESSON LEARNED

The words "I am," can have a tremendous impact on your life. Whether that impact is positive or negative really depends on the meanings you give to the words and how much you internalize that phrase. But just as important are the words that follow that I AM.

Sometimes you have to believe in yourself because if you don't, you make it difficult to allow others to believe in you. As Lisa Nichols (one of the world's most requested motivational speakers, as well as a media personality and corporate CEO whose global platform has reached and served nearly 30 million people), said, "The world is looking at you and following your example of how to treat you." Or as Steve Jobs said, "Sometimes life is going to hit you in the head with a brick. Don't lose faith." If you have goals and dreams written down then you have a much better chance of hitting back at that brick.

Martin Luther King, the American Civil Rights Leader said that, "No person has the right to rain on your dreams." So don't allow anyone to rain on your dreams and even more importantly, please don't rain on your own dreams.

Reflection Questions

1. What examples are you showing the world and how do you want the world to treat you? [How does your language (verbal and body language) invite the world to treat you?]

2. What are the negative "I AM" statements you need to stop using when you speak about yourself? Write them down. You may want to ask supportive friends to listen for your negative "I am" statements and share them with you. Sometimes they are part of a bad habit, and we can't hear them.

3. What I AMs do you need to adopt to improve your life? Ask your supportive friends to listen to them. Do they sound authentic?

4. How could your I AMs impact someone else's life?

5. Who do you influence? For whom are you a role model?

6. Do you have children who you constantly talk negatively in front of?

Chapter Four

BOY GET OFF
MY PIG

"You don't get to choose your family.
They are God's gift to you as you are to them".

—Desmond Tutu

Growing up as a young black boy in St. Matthews, South Carolina had its challenges. I had a wonderful childhood, however, and remember it fondly. Like many other small towns in the south at that time iduring the late 60s and 70s, St Matthews was a town with a population of around one to two thousand people. Downtown was thriving, and my brothers and sisters and I couldn't wait for the weekends when we would dress up and go downtown or to dances at different dance halls. I laugh now because as a child, things always seem larger than they are and this fact is always brought back to me when I visit home these days. Gone are those thriving businesses, just a few shops remain open and everything seems so small.

The town during my youth had two communities separated by a bridge. A white side of the town and a colored side (colored was used to describe African Americans during that era) of town, which is sort of ironic because once the schools were integrated, the schools I attended were on that white side of the town.

While playing on my side of town, the world seemed lively, and at times it didn't seem like I had a care in the world. However, one of the things that have always been difficult for me to understand even now is why we had the separate communities, bathrooms, and water fountains.

This was always a source of disheartenment and amazement to me, and even when I think of it today, even with my logical brain, I cannot understand the thinking behind people being separated simply because of the color of their skin. But as a child, I didn't give it as much thought as perhaps I might have if my childhood hadn't been so wonderful. Besides, my parents made sure we had a relatively normal childhood, whatever that term *normal* means.

One of the highlights each year was that my extended family, cousins, uncles, and aunts would travel down to St. Matthews, South Carolina to visit my grandparents, and all the family would congregate there to celebrate family. Celebrating the fact that we all were still living, the fact that love was plentiful, to remember the past but more importantly, to celebrate my grandparents.

My grandparents lived in the country as we use to call it, on a farm with horses, pigs, cows, with fields of cotton, corn, peas, tomatoes, and okra. Those early morning breakfasts, with grits, eggs, bacon, orange juice, home cooked biscuits with syrup, were wonderful and I can still hear my grandmother now, calling, come and get it while it's hot. Man, I can still smell and see those breakfasts, even after all these years.

Every morning, you could smell the bacon and the biscuits, hear the chickens crow, hear the cows moo and then my grandfather saying to my grandmother, "Buck" (his pet name for my grandmother), "we have a long day ahead," and then give us instructions for the tasks we needed to complete that day.

I can still hear him now saying to me, "Boy, you got to work hard and make good choices if you are going to be successful. And we run a successful household here. And we are successful because everyone plays their part." I would notice my grandmother looking at me with love in her eyes agreeing with my grandfather while she finished her breakfast.

You see, I loved my grandparents and wanted to spend as much time at their home as I possibly could. As a matter of fact, I would come home from high school, drop my books at my parents' home, grab something to eat and then hit the railroad tracks, walking 3 miles out of town just to see and be with them. I did this at least 3 times a week.

Sometimes I would catch the school bus if I didn't have any chores at my parent's house.

On this particular day, we were all there, extended family from New York and Philadelphia, and all we kids were bored. I mean really bored.

The adults were in the house, and all the kids were outside playing on the farm. It was a beautiful day, the sun was shining and a slight wind blowing. So being kids and at this particular time, taking a dare from my cousin Reggie to do something crazy, I noticed the pigs in the hog pen and I decided I was going to ride the biggest one, just to show off. Have you ever done something that you know was just stupid? I mean just outright dumb? No, I mean Dumb!

Because I lived there and I felt it was my second home, I thought what the hell, I can do anything I wanted to do. So, I decided to ride a pig. Yep, you heard me, ride a pig. I decided to ride the pig so I could show off to my cousin.

To top that off, I was really encouraged by the other kids cheering me on. Just remember that I mentioned the word dumb.

However, what I failed to realize was that the particular pig I had decided I was going to ride was pregnant. Big problem. A big problem for the pig, yes it could have been, but a bigger problem for me, yes and a double yes. Not only was I not supposed to ride the pig, but also my problem was compounded by the fact that she was pregnant. I jumped on that pig and was having the ride of my life. Laughing and holding on as best as I could. And of course, I was being cheered on by my cousins. I wonder now, smiling to myself, how dumb could one person have been

While I captured everyone's attention with my activities and everyone was laughing and having fun, the unthinkable happened. My grandfather walked out of the house. He went crazy, "Boy, how damn stupid are you?" By this time, I felt really stupid. He continued, "Don't you realize the pig is pregnant and that this is how we make our living". You see, I never really thought about it that way. To me, it was about having fun and trying to show off. Man, not only was I embarrassed, I just never thought that I was letting my family down or the real impact and significance of the animals to our family.

However, years later, I realized the significance of my actions. You see, that pig represented prosperity for the family, it represented the next meal, and its offspring would produce food for generations to come. The offspring from that pig were money in the bank for my family and the community in terms of them being sold or even used to produce food for my grandfather's business, but more directly, his family which included ME.

So, I guess that day was a huge learning experience for me and one I will never forget. If there was any lesson I learned from it, it's the one lesson which has remained with me even today. And trust me, my family, sisters, brothers, and cousins made sure that I never forget it either. It is the talk that has always come up even to this day when the family gets together. But what is really interesting to me is that even to this day, my grandfather never mentioned the incident again. Not once.

LESSON LEARNED

Life is about working together and making sure all the wheels work together. Or as my grandfather would often say, "If you don't believe in cooperation and people working together, then look at what happens to a wagon when it loses a wheel." Everything has its place and even as a youngster you have to realize that.

Everything you do in your life has consequences. You need to learn to think before you act, and remember that when you are entrusted with others people's dreams, it is critical that you handle those dreams with the utmost care. Yes, even if the family's dream includes a pig.

Reflection Questions

1. What silly act have you committed during your childhood that benefited you as an adult in terms of your learning experiences? Have you been able to share those experiences with others?

2. How are you using that experience to inform your decisions today?

3. How has one lesson you learned during your childhood benefited you in a present-day relationship?

4. Is that silly act still affecting the way you feel today? Your self-esteem for example.

Chapter Five

THE SAXOPHONE MOMENT

"Let's keep it real. You can work as hard as you want, but if you don't work towards a goal with purpose and direction, then you can just forget it.

—**Renaldo Lawrence**

Rosa Caldwell, my grandmother, was one of the best human beings I have ever known and I'm not saying that because she was my grandmother.

I watched her countless number of times cook pies, put them on the kitchen window, and just leave them there to cool, or at least that's what I thought. Rosa would come back and just about each time some of the pies would be gone. While I was always perplexed and quite honestly upset that the pies had disappeared my grandmother was never stressed or upset and I mean NEVER. I used to look in her face and wonder why, but she would look at me smile and say, "God will always make a way."

It was years later that I was told by my mother, that it was my grandmother's way of feeding the children in the community who didn't have a lot of food at home to eat. So, values such as sharing, looking out for other human beings - whether I knew them or not - which I have learned from my grandmother, have played a tremendous part in how I go about my daily life and how I have helped my wife, Janis, in raising our children Andrew and Jessica.

This particular morning, I was at my grandmother's house practicing the saxophone when the phone rang. My grandmother was so encouraging towards anything I did, and playing the saxophone was no different. She had me believing that I was the greatest saxophonist there was. I am convinced that her love and encouragement was one of the main reasons I am confident in myself as a person today. Sometimes you have to live through someone else's vision of you before you realize the greatness in yourself.

My grandmother had me feeling sort of like I was Count Basie. Count Basie was an American jazz pianist, organist, bandleader, and composer who lived from 1904 – 1984. Hey what did I know? I was 14 and as she often said, "A child should always have dreams and goals." My grandmother was always, from the first moment I remembered her, one of the most positive and encouraging individuals I have ever met or had the pleasure to spend any length of time with. And to this day I have been blessed with the lessons she has taught me.

And although she went through years of anguish because of racism, she never mentioned one thing in front of me about racism. As a matter of fact, I have a white wife and my grandmother was more welcoming to her than anyone else. I don't think she saw race in that way. She was just about trying to ensure that her family was safe, fed, and happy. Rosa Caldwell was a special person, one that the world misses and during every day of her life, one of her primary goals was to help others live a well fed, happy, and productive life.

She was one of my biggest fans. As a matter of fact, thinking back now on those times, other than my band instructor, she was my **only** saxophone fan!

I really wanted to learn the sax because it was a very nice sounding instrument. And besides, it drew attention to me and at the age of 14, a long and lanky young man, unsure of my place in the world, it gave me something that I could do that would let people, or at least my few friends, know that this was something I was serious about. Besides, I had just started, really seriously started, noticing girls and I thought they would love me because of my saxophone playing abilities.

I felt that now I had arrived to take my place as a serious individual in the world. A Saxophone King. Hey, I was just 14, what did I know; give me a little credit for trying.

Ok, remember I mentioned that the phone rang? It was my Aunt S from New Jersey. Well, it was my Aunt from the big city. Wow!!! Remember this was in the late 60s, so a phone call was something special. Nothing like the ones you little whippersnappers have today with the texting or the call a minute crowd. It was the rotary dial phone. You actually had to put your finger in this circle on the front of the phone with the number and dial.

My grandmother wanted me to play my sax for my Aunt so this was a huge moment for me. I began to play. Now I had been practicing this piece for quite some time but just couldn't finish the last section of the piece. For some reason, I just couldn't get this section right. When I got to that particular part, my grandmother asked me to stop and praised me for my rendition of the piece I had just completed.

Unbeknown to me at the time, she stopped me just at the part of the music where I had struggled and wasn't sure how to play. She praised me so much to my Aunt S that I felt like a million bucks. It was only later on in my life that I understood just how that was a confidence-building moment for me and also a learning moment. I will never forget the lessons she taught me that day. Ever! I have learned to give praise where praise is due. Sometimes you don't have to climb the whole mountain, but you should be praised for getting started and climbing part of the mountain. Thank you, grandmother.

In your daily journey through your life, there will be opportunities for you to praise people. Please do so because you never know what that word of encouragement will do for their self-esteem.

LESSON LEARNED

It is important to know your craft. If you are not fully prepared, then it might be a good idea to do the research, find the answers and understand the complexities of the situation you are about to embark upon, or in my case, make sure you know or at least try to know your limitations before you tackle a task.

Opportunity can come at any time and being prepared means that you can take advantage of that opportunity at the appropriate time.

But the most important lesson I learned from the moment that I played the saxophone for my Aunt S was to understand that you need to give people a chance. As a leader you need to know and recognise that some people might not have the passion you have for a particular task, or indeed possess a similar work ethic. That doesn't necessarily mean that they won't be an asset to you and your company.

So, in conclusion, I truly believe that in your life, you need to make sure that you go where you are celebrated and not just tolerated, and when you are there, give praise where praise is due. Praising someone takes nothing away from the job you have done. So, praise and appreciate, two words I believe the world needs to embrace more. Please remember, you don't need to tear someone down to make yourself look good or feel better.

Reflection Questions

1. What can you say to someone today which would make their day and which could possibly help give them confidence in themselves? You never know how just a *hello* can help make someone's day. Give it a try, and you just might be pleasantly surprised.

2. Who has helped you through a rough patch in your life? Have you thought of just sending a handwritten card to that person, it could even make their day?

3. Who has been such a great friend that you might want to brighten their day with a phone call or a text?

"True friendships are the siblings God never gave us."
—Mencius

Chapter Six

THE FIRE

"Let's keep it real. You can work as hard as you want, but if you don't work towards a goal with purpose and direction, then you can just forget it."

—Renaldo Lawrence

When you are growing up, friendships mean the world to you, having friends plays such a big part in helping you develop your self-esteem. The thought that some other person wants to hang out with you is the ultimate confirmation that you have arrived.

Growing up, I had such a friend in Clint. Clint was a person who I really connected with from the first time we met. Both of our fathers were friends and saw each other often, so, this really helped cement our relationship.

Clint was also the first person my age I knew with a job making real money, so man, he was automatically my hero.

Clint and I spent so much time together and shared so many positive memories.

However, one of the most impactful moments I have ever had in my life is what I will call the fire incident. Can I ask how many of you have ever been silly enough to play with matches, or even dumber, play with matches with a friend, in a field of dried grass and corn, on a 100-degree day? Huh? I'm waiting for your answers. Well, I have! Yeah, really brainy, right?

Let me paint you a picture. It was a bright and sunny day as most of the days in South Carolina are during the summers. My father was at work; mom was in the house doing household chores, and all of my younger brothers and sisters were either in the house or visiting their friends.

The day started as most of them do, getting up, having breakfast, and as a young boy of 14 wondering what the world had in store for me that day. In other words, bored out of my mind. For some reason, this day my friend Clint came round much earlier to see me at my home and being the bored souls we were, we decided to play a game. A game that in hindsight was not the smartest thing we had done in our lives. Or as I discovered, just about the dumbest thing I had ever done in my life. Who said I needed or wanted a best friend?

We were walking in a field right across from my house that consisted of extremely dried grass and corn. In South Carolina in the summer the temperature gets up around 100 degrees, and that's before midday. The grass and corn were golden brown and extremely dry.

So, there we were, bored, in 100 degree weather (please keep that point in mind) making a decision to strike matches and throw them onto the field. The intention was that when we threw the flaming matches down we would immediately stamp on them to prevent a fire from starting. Really smart.

Well, to say the least, we failed. The next thing I knew when I looked up from the field was that there was a huge fire burning completely out of control. Then all of a sudden, as I turned to look at Clint, I saw flashing lights coming towards me and before I knew it, every fire truck and police car in St. Matthews was there. Wow, the whole police and fire department. Someone in the neighborhood had called the fire and police department; so at least somebody was being sensible. . . . because we surely weren't.

Now I have done some dumb things in my life, but this must rank as number one on my list as a teenager. Oh, I would have many more mistakes as an adult, but that's another story. To make matters even worse, when the fire became uncontrollable, my good friend Clint, ran to tell my mother. He forgot all about helping me put the fire out and wanted to look after his best interests.

Best friend, huh? Maybe a re-evaluation of our friendship was in order.

Well, as you probably guessed, my mother wasn't too happy about the situation. In attendance at my 'event' was a whole police department, the town's fire brigade, and of course just about everyone else in St. Matthews. If they didn't know me before, well they would know me now. This was not the way I wanted the public from St. Matthews, or any other town, to know me to be honest with you. The situation became a little (to say the least) overwhelming, and I felt that the situation left me with only one option. I did the logical thing.

I ran. Oh, man, did I run.

Remember now, I was 14 years old, so I wasn't the wisest or brightest spark in the world. The field was on fire 30 yards from my house now, so I ran to the house and hid under the chimney, where I was absolutely sure no one would ever, ever think to look for me. Safe. Or so I thought.

Well, lo and behold, remember that best friend Clint? Turns out he was all too happy to tell my mother exactly where I was. Not only that, my best friend gave her the whole story.

The whole story.

No need to think whether I should re-evaluate my friendship now. I was completely through with Clint as a friend; well, at least for the next three days anyway.

[**Side note** – Growing up I was whipped four times in my life, all by my mother. And man, I will tell you, I deserved every one of them. For three of them, I had to do the dreaded walk. I can hear my mother now, "Boy go and get me a switch from that tree." That always seemed to be like the longest walk in history. Of course, it was, because I made sure I took my sweet time hoping she would change her mind. No such luck.

With the switch in hand, I went back to my waiting mother. Although I got a whipping only four times, I learned from the first one to never try and explain why I did what I did during the whipping process. You see, in black families, or at least the black families I grew up with, when you are getting a whipping, you need to learn to shut up and never comment on the licks you are receiving.

An example; when the first lick comes, you always try and explain and justify that you won't do the deed again, big mistake. I learned from my previous experience that every time I received a lick to be quiet, otherwise my mom would use what I said and add, "I… Know. You… Wont. Do. It. Again," to the end of my sentence. Every syllable, every word would be an extra lick. My parents had different parenting styles, and it was really funny because my father never whipped me a day in his life. He had another technique he used which was powerful. All my dad had to say to me was, "So that is how much you think of me then?" Man, those words destroyed me every time. So much so that I have never spanked my children. I just used my father's method, and to my great relief, it worked every time. But you know what's really funny, I have often thanked my mom for those whippings. I learned a lot, and I believe that they helped me to understand right from wrong. It is really funny now when I speak with my brothers and sisters about those experiences, and we laugh, but man I tell you what, it wasn't a laughing matter when it was happening. Those whippings were not fun, well not for me anyway, I never really asked my mom about her opinion about it.]

Now back to the fire story.

This whipping, however, was different from the others because I didn't have to do the dreaded walk, my mother was all too happy to just bring her belt out of hiding. Man, did I get it that day. But what I will always remember is how much I let my mother down, how embarrassed she felt and the look of disappointment on her face.

So, the story ended with the police and firefighters making sure the fire was out, and everyone was safe and sound. As for me, well after the realization of what we had done, notice I said we, I could see how much of a mistake we had made and I was really and truly sorry about the incident. Luckily enough, no one was hurt and, even better for me, my mom didn't have to pay for any of the damages. Clint and I? Well, after three days we were friends again and just laughed and laughed about what had happened. Oh, and even though I was laughing so hard it took me a few days before I could sit down comfortably. Thanks, Pernell

LESSON LEARNED

It is important to understand that life is about living and working with others, and destroying other people's property is not the way to go. I learned my lesson that day and I guess the moral of this tale is that one, you shouldn't play with matches, and two, you really need to think about what you are about to do and how your actions may affect others.

Something serious could have happened that day and I would have never forgiven myself. I guess in a funny sort of way also, you need to think about the people you are associating yourself with. Are their decisions the best ones for you? I know our decision was not the best decision we could have made on this day.

Reflection Questions

1. Do you really think about the consequences before you make your decisions or do you go head first and let the chips fall where they may?

2. Do you have people around you who are making good decisions for the both of you or just themselves?

3. What fires have you had to put out that has impacted your life for both the positive and negative?

Chapter Seven

TIME

"Like sand through an hourglass, these are the days of our lives."

—Unknown

There is, or used to be a show on TV that started out with the phrase, "Like sand through an hourglass, these are the days of our lives," and I wonder now where some of my days have gone. I remember when I use to sit around and think, man, *my grandmother and mother are old.* Then I was 18, and before I knew it, I was 21. It seemed like within a short span of time I was 30 and during those years some of my friends and family disappeared from the earth. And I thought, where have my days gone? Before I knew it, I was 40, and then 50, and they were calling me old. But it seemed like a moment ago that I was that little boy. "Like sand through an hourglass, these are the days of our lives."

Life has an amazing way of creeping up on you. I once heard a man say that youth is wasted on the young. You only really realize what it means when your time has slipped by or is slowly slipping through the hourglass of your life, and you wake up one day and think man, how old am I?

So, you ask yourself what am I going to do now? "The world seems to be passing me by," my aunt once said to me. I'm going to tell you what I told her. My exact words to her were, "I'll tell you what you are going to do, you are going to live. Yes, live. Live for all the days you have lived before, live for all the knowledge, experience, and wisdom you have gained over the past years and use that wisdom, knowledge, and experience to not only help yourself but to help benefit the world." That world can be right there in your neighborhood or your community. There is no way you can tell me that with all that you have in your life in terms of knowledge, experience, and wisdom, and with over 7 billion people in the world you have nothing to offer to someone. I don't believe it, and if you really think about it seriously, you don't believe it either.

Because I tell you what, so many people need you. Need you for maybe a single word of encouragement, a simple hello or even a simple meal. There is someone who needs what you have to give.

Imagine with all the personal tools you have developed over the years, the tools that help you deal with all the different situations you've encountered day to day, even the tools you have developed to survive and prosper over the last month or year. Tools such as the ability to be patient, the ability to cope with different situations, and the ability to work through financial and relationship difficulties. Just think of the value you can bring to the world; but there is one catch. You must believe that you have something of value to give to the world. Observe your environment, look for opportunities to help others by smiling at a stranger, smiling at your wife, your husband. Or how about just smiling within yourself while permitting yourself to feel good because you have made it this far in life. My mother, Pernell once said, "If you are against yourself, then you have no chance to be or feel successful."

Live for you. Live for all those grains of sand that will continue to trickle down through the hourglass slowly. But for each drop of sand that falls, understand that it is for his glory that you were given the opportunity to live. Think of all the people you have loved and lost, but you are still here. This can only mean that he has a major purpose for your life and regardless of the age and stage you are in your life, it is the gift that you have been given that holds your purpose.

So, get up and live, live in your gift and your purpose. Trust me some people need what you have. They need that knowledge, and they need the benefit of all that experience and wisdom you have to give.

I will always remember when my grandmother was 83 years and in a nursing home. During one of our many conversations, she said to me, "I am 83 years old, and I still feel like that little girl of 15." I thought wow, I still feel like I am 15. What a blessing. It was almost like she had gone full circle.

There is a quote that I love and think is so fitting. It reads, "Never think that what you have to offer is insignificant. There will always be someone out there who needs what you have to give."

Nothing is ever wasted unless you don't use it. So, my question to you is this, "What are you going to do with the time you have left?" Don't miss the opportunity to have the best time of your life and in the process, change the quality of someone else's life. Let those grains of sand stand for something more than yourself. So please believe in what you want to do, love it and work to accomplish all of your goals. Why not? The world needs you!

LESSON LEARNED

There is one thing I know for sure, and that is that everyone has value on this earth, from the child who is one year old to the lady or gentlemen who is 100 years old. For it is the one year old who reminds us how wonderful it is to have life, to be dependent on another, and to show us what love really feels like, and the 100-year-old, who can give you the simplest advice which can help change your perspective, and in turn could have a chance to influence you to the point of you being able to change the world.

It is the blessings that each of us have been given as human beings that we get to grow, gain experience, then use that experience to help others prosper, to make our society a place where all of us can be happy and whole. It is "Like sand through an hourglass, and these are truly the days of your life." What are you going to do with your sand?

Reflection Questions

1. What goals and dreams do you have that you want
    to accomplish?

2. Finish this sentence… like sand through the hourglass, these…

3. What is your gift? How will you use that gift to brighten up
    your world?

4. Are you living in your past? Do you need to catch up and live
    in your present?

5. Are you having a pity party? If so, what can you do to start celebrating
    your life?

Remember that when you change a simple thought, it is possibly to
change a life. Yep, just by a simple thought and decision.

Chapter Eight

GROWING UP

"The greatest gift of life is friendship, and I have received it."
—**Hubert Humphrey**

GROWING UP IN in St. Matthews, South Carolina, there is no way you could have told me that a skinny little black kid would reach the heights I have. This is why I always try and tell my students about my past life and how in those days education wasn't important to me. And then I always try and illustrate how I made the switch in terms of my mental approach towards education.

Most of the students that I teach need role models, and even if this is something they don't realize, they seem happy to listen to my story.

Between my background and theirs, even if there is sometimes a subtle difference, the students can totally relate to my story. But to get to that comfort zone with them, it is important that I allow them to be themselves in the classroom. Allow them to express themselves but with control and respect. Part of my goal I believe is to help them understand that there is a rainbow at the end of the tunnel if you work hard enough.

It might not be as big a rainbow as the next person's, but if you are happy, then that is truly what matters. But being 14, 15 or 16, it is hard to understand your place in the world. It is hard to figure out what value you bring to the other people, but more importantly, I believe it is hard to even know who you really are. Having someone you can relate to helps you to chart a path to what's possible to help you understand your place in the world. And just as important, they could help you understand who you might become.

For me, the whole process starts with respect; respect for me, for themselves and for other students in the classroom.

My mother struggled to take care of her six kids, but did an incredible job of raising extremely well balanced children. My father left home later in my life, earlier in my siblings' lives; however, all of us made a great life for ourselves. This is the message I wish to stress to my students in every conversation, whether in a group or individually.

There are times that I will arrange meeting with students just to share a story about issues I have had in my life. But the key to my stories is that they always relate to something that I know the students are either going through or have gone through. Examples of my stories include: If their father has left them at some point in their lives, how they are making money, if they are a one parent family and how they can deal with those issues. And I don't mind telling them how I have dealt with those issues in my own life. Being honest with issues, students can see that you are a real-life person who also has feelings. The issues I have are many and this allows me to really engage with my students. So, when the student or students are ready to let go and talk, I am always ready to listen. Always, because I have been there when I didn't have anyone to talk with and it is not a pleasant feeling when you have feelings inside of you and no way to get them out. But again, everything should be done with sensitivity, dignity, and a proper understanding of how far it is possible take a potentially delicate discussion.

Going to High School, in St Matthews, South Carolina, playing basketball, gaining a basketball scholarship, to Appalachian State University, playing for a Hall of Fame coach, Bobby Cremins, and being drafted by the LA Clippers.

Would you believe that I started out with going to an outhouse at my grandmother's house? An outhouse! Would you believe that I remember the colored drinking water fountains? Would you believe that I was someone who didn't understand my place in life?

While at my grandmother's earlier on in my life, I had to go outside to use the bathroom. Do you hear me? An outhouse. I truly know that by remembering and thinking about my life, anything can be accomplished if you believe and try to do the right thing.

Being cut from the LA Clippers, then playing basketball in South America for two years, traveling to play in Finland for two years, Argentina for a year, and then a few countries inbetween, and then England; traveling the world doing what I loved to do. I'm from St. Matthews SC. A town that has two major traffic lights. Blessing, blessing, and blessings. This wasn't supposed to happen to me, or at least that is what the statistics say for an African American man in America in my position.

I could never have imagined this could have happened. I thought basketball was just for enjoyment, something that allowed me to make a living. But no, God was using basketball to prepare me for a bigger goal, A larger and more significant goal. which would impact the world and many lives.

To have the opportunity to work in schools where I can engage students, be a role model and directly impact lives, well, there is no better way for me to live my life and on top of that to write this book. Do you hear me? But I will tell you that every time opportunity knocked, I made sure I was prepared for it, when I wasn't, I made sure that I explained why; when the opportunity came around again, I completely knocked it out of the park. Completely!

To be one of the world's authorities on eLearning in the educational sector. Are you kidding me? This skinny little kid is helping change the world. The boy who hated school? The boy who hoped that the teacher would never call on him to answer a question in class? Wow!

People, I'm telling you, to be an Adobe Educational Leader, Lynda. com author, LinkedIn author, an Apple Distinguished Educator, Microsoft Innovator Teacher, and Teacher Developer, where I can help impact teachers' lives and in turn, they can, through my courses, learn how they can have the opportunity to impact millions of students' lives. Me? Are you serious?

And all I did was to start off by doing what was necessary and filling a need. I did what was possible, and then all of a sudden, I woke up and I was doing the impossible.

I really believe that anyone can reach their goals, but there is a process. And that process will take a lot of time, but it is possible to make it happen. You just have to believe. What other reasonable choice is there? And you know what, it doesn't matter how old you are or at what stage in your life.

To get the process started here are some steps you can take:

1. Find a place that you feel comfortable. I like to find a place where I feel creative, and to me, there is no place better than Starbucks. Internet access, tables, and most of all great coffee. Now, sit down and relax.

2. Think hard and try and discover what you really want. You have to know what you want if you ever wish to get there. Think through your life and try to think about what you would do and enjoy even if you weren't paid for it.

3. Write it down. This is so important because it will give you your measuring stick. You can always read about your journey while trying to reach your destination. Trust me, there will be times when life slaps you in the face, and if you don't have it written down, your goals might take a totally different path. That's if you remember them at all. The other thing about writing your goals down is that you may see an opportunity right in front of you that you missed because you were too consumed with your own problems or tasks.

4. Set some targets and then find a way to measure yourself for each step you have specified. This is critical because without measurement or tracking, nothing gets done. Find someone who has done what you want to do and model their actions. This will help cut down on the whole process.

5. Lastly, you must have a strong, positive self-image to help prepare you for success. And you do this by being the best at your craft in your chosen field. So much so that they cannot get rid of you even if they wanted to. To help you with this process, go back and read numbers three and four.

Get a plan, write it down, apply action towards accomplishing your goals and then watch how truly magical it is when your goals and dreams are written on paper, where you can read them daily, two or three times, and watch how things just start to happen. In the beginning, it might be that you just feel good about completing one task towards a goal. But soon momentum will start, and you will be off to the races.

But please remember that, as Leah Labelle said, "Work hard for what you want because it won't come without a fight. You have to be strong and courageous and know that you can do anything you put your mind to. If someone puts you down or criticizes you, just keep on believing in yourself and turn it into something positive." But you have to write it down, I cannot stress this enough. Put it in your bathroom, in your car, the tool shed, the kitchen, your desk at home, your desk at work, everywhere you can see it. Start small because we all need wins, regardless of how small, to help encourage us. Master one thing at a time, always looking and thinking about how each part of your dreams or goals will connect to make a whole.

If you try to do too much too soon, you will become discouraged and that does you no good or anyone who you hope to accomplish your goal for. One last thing, you may want to be careful who you wish to tell your dreams to. Not everyone will understand your goals and dreams. So, like picking your dearest friends, be careful who you tell you dearest hopes and dreams to.

LESSON LEARNED

I spent a lot of my past life thinking about being successful, accomplishing goals such as writing a book, but I never did anything about it. Yeah, all the basketball was fantastic, but at some point and time in your life you need to move on. I have friends who continually talk about yesterday, and that's cool, but we need to look at the future. What past event are you still living? Would it help you to write your goals down along with deadlines for their accomplishments to help you envision your future?

It is essential that you think about what you want, set goals and write them down. Rome wasn't built in a day and it never would have been built at all without a dream, vision, and the guts to just get started.

Do you have the guts to get started? Well, do you? Your life and your family life can depend on it.

"If opportunity doesn't knock, build a door."-
—Milton Berle

Reflection Questions

1. What can you do today to make your loved ones know that you appreciate them?

2. Have you written down the steps to help you envision your goals?

3. Do you have your goals written on every surface in your house, your car, so that you are constantly reminded of what you are trying to accomplish?

Remember that you have two choices. One, write it down along with a roadmap so that you can see where you are trying to get to. Second way, go to work every day, come home and just dream about what your life can be. But just remember this, every day that goes by is one less day for you to celebrate your success and your family success. Your choice.

Chapter Nine

LIVING WITH PAST REGRETS

"Sometimes it is imperative to look back over your past. It has been said that without some knowledge of your past, it is impossible to construct a meaningful future."

—Renaldo Lawrence

Living with past regrets can be tough, and if you are not careful over a period of time, the regrets can wear you out both physically and mentally. So, every once in a while you have to check yourself.

Sometimes in life, you go through situations in which you have no control. One such earth-shaking event took place in my life when I was 18 years ago.

I loved my father dearly, and he was to me, as I think most fathers are to young boys who have fathers at home, my hero. We adore them, and regardless of how they act sometimes, we still love them. Some of us see our fathers every day; they go to work, come home, play with us, and apply discipline when they think it is necessary.

The one thing you learn about your father as you grow older, however, is that he is not that superhero that you thought he was as a child. You discover that he has strengths and weakness like everyone else. But I think the thing that really strikes you as a kid is that your father is vulnerable. Just like any human being you will come across. The other thing I will say is that through my fathere's vulnerability I saw how to be a man, the good and the bad.

It was a Friday afternoon, and I had just driven back to St. Matthews S.C. Man, home for the weekend from Lancaster S.C, where I played Junior College basketball. Basketball at that time was my life and every decision I made in some way revolved around it. That afternoon after I got home, I said my hellos, and ate dinner. During a family conversation, my mother told me that my father was in the hospital. The doctors, she said, didn't think it was that serious. So I thought it was a routine visit even though he had to stay in the hospital.

Although my dad was in hospital, he did have a request for me; could I drop by and give him a shave. I remember thinking that this was not a problem and I could do it on Saturday. I was looking forward to it because I had not seen him in a while. My mom and I agreed that Saturday would be a good day.

It was a Friday night and that Saturday I had nothing planned, all I needed to do was a small piece of coursework which would take me minutes tops. I will never forget how beautiful it was on that Saturday morning. In my mom's house, she was usually up early, just like my grandmother, cooking breakfast. You could hear the birds singing, the sun was shining brightly, and I got up that day without a care in the world. And man, you could smell the bacon and biscuits. Just like my grandmother used to make.

I was just happy to be home for some of my mom's cooking (and to see my brothers and sisters). Priceless! Man, that woman can cook. Some of my friends who would often come over for breakfast used to say, that my mom's food was so good that it made you want to slap your mother. One of my friends, Dooley, still comes over every week even when I am not there. That was just a phrase to illustrate just how good the food was. I laugh now when I think of the comments because I can hear my friends saying it.

Around noon that day, I had a phone call from one of my friends mentioning that there was going to be a basketball game on Saturday afternoon and all the top players from the area were going to be there.

You have to understand that when it came to basketball for me, the whole idea was to be the best basketball player I could be. In order to be the best basketball player in South Carolina I felt that you had to play and practice against the very best players as often as possible.

That way, you not only had bragging rights but you had a gauge of just how good you were.

Well, this Saturday was my opportunity to prove myself to the other players, but even more importantly, to myself. You see, I heard so much about these players and knew that if I played well, it would enhance my reputation; on top of that give me more confidence as a young kid playing basketball. It was always about reputation. Always. Like a young gunslinger from the Wild West riding into town to slay the big bad gunslinger.

In my case, however, it was to prove myself once more against these amazing basketball players who were local heroes. "I couldn't miss this game," I said to myself. It is amazing how you can rationalize and make anything fit your will and desire if you really want to. *My dad is good and he would understand just how important this game is to me.* Yeah, he will get it, I thought. It won't be a problem.

I played very well that day and was so proud of myself. I now knew I was just as good a player as anyone else in the state of South Carolina. Not only did I think I played well, but the fact was that my peers also acknowledged that I did. So, I jumped in my car and drove back home. The journey took no more than 25 minutes.

As I approached the house I could tell something was wrong. My father didn't even enter my mind as I drove up to the house. My mom was on the porch as I approached the house. My mom is the most straight-talking person I know, and she doesn't hold back her punches. So when Pernell spoke, she got straight to the point. "Boo," this was my nickname, "your father died, your dad is dead." You know when someone tells you something, and it doesn't register straight away, well, this was the feeling I had at that moment. All I could think of was that, man, I was supposed to go and shave my dad. Oh, man, I was supposed to go and shave my dad. I cannot tell you how I felt that moment. When I finally realized what Pernell had said, it felt like a kick in the stomach. It would take me ten years not to feel so guilty about not seeing my father that day. Ten whole years and even now, thirty nine years later I still think of it. But everything works for his goodness. Everything!

As I write these words now, I have forgiven myself, a long time ago, for not visiting my dad. But as I said, it took me ten years to realize that life is about chances and opportunities and sometimes, sadly, missed opportunities. I missed the opportunity to see my father that day but how was I to know that it would be the last chance I would ever have to see him, to shave him. There is one thing that I do know, however, and that is, it was all meant to be, and I wasn't supposed to see my father before his death. I really believe that, and through prayer and reading my Bible, coming to that conclusion was hard, but one that I think is the right one. I really do, from the bottom of my heart. So, I'm in a good place about the situation, and I really believe that I wasn't supposed to see him.

I'm good knowing that I loved him and he loved me, but also that sometimes having regrets gets you nowhere. Mitch Albom's quote sums it up for me when he says, "Death ends a life, not a relationship." Death ends a life, not a relationship.

So even to this day, I have and will always have that precious relationship with my father.

Always!

LESSON LEARNED

I believe that we need to use our gifts of life and happiness to help each other grow and to help each other realize that all of us have missed opportunities, but we shouldn't let them define or discourage us, only learn from them regardless of the pain and suffering at that moment.

So, live your life, live your life with passion, breathe each moment, taste each of the precious moments you have been given, but more importantly, allow your greatness to bless others who may come across your path. Did you hear that, allow your greatness to bless others who may come across your path.

We must not just go through life existing day to day, where we don't even remember what we did the previous day. We need to feel our days, feel the love that exists between us and other human beings, feel what it is really like to get up in the morning and live. Feel the work we do each day and make it mean something, not only for you but the workers around you, to the world, and most importantly, we need to feel the love we have for ourselves and the precious gift of life we have been given.

Please remember that sometimes we weren't meant to be there, and that doesn't mean we are a good or bad person, it just means that we are human beings who have vulnerabilities.

"We must let go of the life we have planned,
so as to accept the one that is waiting for us."
—Joseph Campbell

Reflection Questions

1. What are you doing the same each day that you could change and which would impact your life in a positive way? Just because you do it, doesn't mean you are benefitting from it. What are your patterns?

2. What have you always wanted to do with your life that your thoughts said you couldn't do?

3. Has your situation changed where it is now possible to accomplish those goals?

4. Are you just existing each day or living life to the fullest?

Write down your answers, you will be surprised at how your reasoning skills will improve when you can see your thoughts written down in front of you. This is the first step to freedom, your freedom, and isn't that what you really want, your personal freedom?

Chapter Ten

PATH TO A VISION

"Boo, come here."

That's what my father used to call me when he was living. You see, as a child regardless of everything else, regardless of what anyone else thought, my father was my hero. As a young boy, he was my guidepost, my leadership destination as a boy, my path to a vision which I had no idea existed. No idea what that vision was and what it could or would be.

On this particular day, my father, Andrew Lawrence, wanted me to ride on his truck to deliver soft drinks to his company's customers. My dad was a driver for Coca-*Cola w*hich to me at the time was like so darn Kool. I cannot tell you how happy, privileged, and blessed I felt that day just to be hanging out with my dad.

As I look back now, I understand just how important moments like this were to both my development as a young man and my ability to feel comfortable in the world. As a young boy, you think you have an eternity to live your life. An eternity to do whatever you want, be the person you hope to become, and you believe (as a matter of fact, you don't give it a second thought as a kid because you think your parents will live forever) you should be.

It was important because that man, my father, in some ways is the blueprint for everything I would hope to become and who I have become. As a young boy, I tried to remember all the good times and there were many of those good times. But there were also bad times and, as I have learned in life, you take the positives use them and move on. As a young boy, growing up during the 60s with the racial tension, a black man did the best he could in the South. And seeing my father and how he handled everything, I now look back and I understand that he did the best he could with both the times he lived in and his education as a man. So, from him, I take the positives he has passed on and share that positiveness with all the people I come in contact with in some form or fashion.

But it is also extremely important that you don't forget the negatives because some of that negativity will be your guidepost for goodness, your barometer to help you sift the good from the bad. For without the negativity, my father would not have been a real man. And a real man shows his weakness and as a young man, although at the time you don't want to see that because you see it as a weakness, you learn later in your life that it is a tremendous asset. It took me a while to learn that; as a matter of fact, I didn't learn that until I had children of my own.

Once you have children of your own, you look back and realize just why your parents did certain things. You realize that for the most part, they did the best they could, at least in my circumstance this is what I believe.

One of the lessons my father taught me was that regardless of what someone thought of you, you have to be yourself and have your own values. Your values are what will sustain you when you have hard times, they will allow and help you make decisions that will be beneficial to all concerned, but most of all, your values will be your goal post for a productive life.

However, my father or mother were not the only ones who were making a difference in my life and helping provide the goal posts for success.

I really believe that it takes a village to raise a child properly. A village where people are responsible for each other, and just because I am not your child or cousin, you care enough about me as a human being to help ensure that I am doing the right thing.

The greatest lessons I learned are the ones which were taught to me by my parents and grandparents, mainly because I have been able to pass on the wisdom and knowledge I gained from them to my children. But make no mistake about it, life has many teachers if you just open your eyes and observe. My blessings are that I had many teachers and that every one of them genuinely cared about me.

So, I have received what I love to call my triple blessings. I have been blessed to have my parents, grandparents, and all the elderly people in St. Matthews who have been a guidepost for me, my values, and my development. So now it is time for me to pass on the baton, to bless others in ways that enhance all of our lives. What about you?

Has my life been smooth? By no stretch of the imagination, but I tell you what, without the knowledge and wisdom I gained from the negative times, I would have made many more mistakes, so I truly appreciate the lessons learned.

SOME OF THOSE VALUES INCLUDE:

1. Being able to stand up, admit your mistakes, and if possible do something to correct the situation.

2. Help as many people as you can during your life's journey. My grandmother used to always say, "Every dog has its day. You never know when your day will run out and you need a helping hand."

    So, help as many people as you can, but do it from your heart, and God will bless you ten times over." My grandmother, man I tell you that women had wisdom even beyond her years and through other members of my family and me, that wisdom will continue to be passed down through generations to come. Your life gets better when you can find a way to share it with someone else.

3. Understand your worth. One of the problems I think we have today is that people don't really understand their worth and value to the world. Each person has value and something to give to the world. It can be as simple as a good word to someone or even help someone complete a chore. Growing up, especially watching my grandfather and how he demonstrated to me that he understood his worth and value every day, through the way he walked, the decisions he made for both himself and the family, and through his I AMs (see chapter 3). My father also used to tell me that if you as a man gave your word to someone, it was your duty to make sure you held your part of the bargain.

4. Live life to the fullest. You never know what challenges you are going to face, so you need to enjoy the time you have. Some of those challenges you can prepare for and others you have to deal with as they appear. So, stay humble, praise your God, smile as much as possible, love like you have never loved before, but most of all, be grateful while making sure you spare some room in your heart and life to help make someone else's life special.

LESSONS LEARNED

Being able to stand up and admit your mistakes is everything. You can only be a role model and person of your word I believe, when you can stand up, look at yourself in the mirror or whoever it is in the face and admit that you have made a mistake. To me, this is a huge step in becoming successful. But it is not just about your success, it is about helping others catch the train along with you. It is about making sure others learn and grow and in the process, trying to stay as positive as possible.

I believe that the whole process is about having a productive life that enhances the world as you see it and the people in it.

Reflective Questions

1. What values have you learned from your family or others to help you reach your goals?

2. Is there someone you can model yourself after who has done the things you are trying to do? Have you looked or are you walking in blind faith?

3. What are your guideposts for your life?

Remember that if it is going to happen, you have to make it happen. Stand up, march forward, and conquer every dream you really want to conquer and accomplish.

> *"Forgiveness is about empowering yourself*
> *rather than empowering your past."*
> **—TD Jakes**

Chapter Eleven

WINNING A LOTTERY

"Forgiveness is about empowering yourself rather than empowering your past."

—T D Jakes

In my opinion, being born in this world is like winning a lottery. However, you never know what side of the lottery you will be born into. When you are involved in the lottery, and all of us are, we have the chance to win anything from one cent to millions or billions of dollars. . . . or whatever currency you want to think of.

But during our conversation, I am not talking about currency, at least not the type you can spend.

I am not thinking of monetary currency. I am talking about the parents' lottery. A lot of us are very lucky, and there are so many of us who are not. There are no perfect families because there are no perfect people. Each of us has our flaws and faults, and during the process of life, each of us has issues which help influence the people around us in both a positive or negative way. Each of us has to make a choice regardless of how our family treats us or regardless of what we didn't get from our parents. It is up to you to make a life for yourself now. The past is the past, and regardless of how hard it is to deal with at times, all of us need to move on. My grandmother often used to say to us kids, "If it is going to be, then it is up to me." So yes, regardless of what your situation was or is, it is up to you to improve it.

During my family life, I remember the arguments between my mom and dad and the arguments between my grandparents. However, most of all, I remember the love between each of them. There are no perfect relationships, and the more I live, the more I think that whatever happens between people, we should learn to not only love but to appreciate each other to the point that we really respect each other.
I don't mean respect with the kindness theme; I mean respect because of our understanding of the trials and tribulations we have gone through together during our relationship. The love, the hate, the toleration, the need, the understanding, the misunderstanding, and to

be honest, the wanting to walk away sometimes thinking that there is something better.

We need a sort of respect that understands each other's needs, each other's love, and that human spirit that tries to help us ensure that humanity will prevail. I will always remember what my mother, Pernell used to tell us; she used to say, "Regardless of the situation you find yourself in, be it negative or positive, it is about how you view that situation over a period of time which can help you determine your destiny."

I truly believe that this statement is right, your beliefs combined with your environment will help determine your destiny. Your destiny. Do you understand that simply changing your environment and mind can change your whole life? Well, do you? The prodigal son was in a hog pen and all of a sudden, he came to himself, surrounded by swine and he made up his mind and came to himself. Then the most amazing thing happened to him. Hear me; the most important thing happened to him. He came to himself and made a DECISION. What decision have you made? Or, more importantly, what decision do you need to make? A changed mind will help you see the world differently, allow you to see yourself differently, and most importantly, allow you to change the world in ways which will enable the people you influence, to influence others.

The next time you are with your friends, just be quiet and listen. Notice the level of complaining. Is this what you want for the rest of your life? No, I know it is not. Or at least I don't think so. Sometimes you have to re-evaluate your friendship groups if you want to get ahead and prosper. But it depends a lot on how much you want to get ahead.

That is the difference between your family and friends, you choose your friends, but not your family. Do you notice that a lot of your family and friends have the "victim mentality?" Everyone is against them. Nothing ever goes their way, and even better, the world owes them a debt.

Where has this attitude gotten them? Most of the time nowhere and nothing but heartache. Trust me, I was there. I used to think that the world owed me a living, but I have learned that the world owes me absolutely nothing. You have to give to get, and this is something your friend with the "victim mentality" never seems to understand.

My grandmother once said this to me, "If you are traveling in one direction for a long period of time, and nothing positive happens, do you change or continue on the same path?"

The way I see it, if you truly want change in your life, you have to turn around, be honest with yourself, and then move forward. The most important thing is that you have a goal and some dreams along with a vision to help propel you forward. For instance, I wanted to write this book. My vision was this book being finished. I am a person who loves to see what other people have created, so I purchased a few books by people I respected so that I could have them right in front of me. By having the books in front of me, my vision and resolve would remain strong. Now to make that vision a reality, I need to take some steps in the right direction.

So, the first thing I did was to write down that goal. Then I wrote down my schedule to see where the gaps were with my time. I then resolved that for one hour a day for four weeks, I would totally commit to writing something. I didn't care at that moment what it was; I knew that I had to train myself to be disciplined enough to write. The stories would come, but the discipline of just being in a single spot and then just writing was my challenge. I then had to figure out the best time to write when I would be totally engaged in the process. This turned out for me to be in the morning because my mind was alert, I love the morning before anyone else gets up. So, this became my writing time. Things started off very slowly but it was my why and the vision of my book being completed that drove me, not excluding being honest with myself about my life.

When I look at the various books I have bought, look at the names of the people who wrote them, I began to wonder why I should be writing a book. Who am I to think that someone else would want to read a book from me? Remember, doubts come to all of us, and it is how you deal with those doubts at that moment that could make the difference between you accomplishing your goal or not. Well, I said to myself the devil is a lie, so like the prodigal son, I came to myself and realized that those authors were people just like me.

But then something else came to my mind that I was taught in grade school and that was that, *"We hold these truths to be self-evident, that all men are created equal, that they are endowed by their Creator with certain unalienable Rights, that among these are Life, Liberty and the pursuit of Happiness."* With these thoughts in mind, there was no way that I wasn't going to write this book.

That is a lesson I have learned. It doesn't matter who they are or what they do; they wake up in the mornings, go to the bathroom just like I do, and have different life issues just like I do. With these thoughts in mind, my focus was never a problem.

Did I have obstacles while writing the book? Of course I did, but you know what? The vision was too bright, and the goal was all important to my why, so that I didn't care what happened, I was going to write. Purpose, vision, why, and goals. You see, it was and is important that my children, nieces, nephews, family members and the world understand that if it hasn't happened for you, could it possibly be that you haven't made an effort to get it done. Whatever **that** it is.

What did I do when I couldn't write? Well, I recorded notes on my phone, and I always have, and still do to this day, carry paper and pencil with me. Even if I am shopping with my wife, on a bus, at a coffee shop or just about anywhere, I have either my phone or pencil and paper because you never know when an idea is going to hit you. How else do I manage to stay focus? Great question. There are two primary ways that I stay focused. One is by writing down what I want to accomplish so I can see it every day. I write it on my phone, on paper, and place it in my office and every place else that I visit on a regular basis.

The other way that I stay focused is to constantly listen to positive podcasts; people like Joel Osteen, Eric Thomas, TD Jakes, and Tony Robbins to name but a few.

Each one of these has written books that have proved to me it is possible to achieve whatever dream and desires you have. But you have to have vision, work hard, and have laser focus and perseverance. Sometimes you have to have what I like to call a mastermind group. None of the people I mentioned above knows who I am, but that doesn't matter. They create and put out content to the world which happens to be relevant to me and my goals, and I can consume it anytime I desire. As a matter of fact, I listen to these gentlemen every day. Morning, midday, and evening. It is what allows me to stay focused and keep my priorities in order. My own personal mastermind group.

Constantly listening to these guys and having my vision and goals in front of me allows me to be truly committed. So, in conclusion, find out what you are truly committed to accomplishing, make sure you know and understand your why, and finally, do the following.

1. Write down your goals and vision.

2. Get yourself a calendar and schedule when you are going to work on your dreams. Make your dreams a burning desire and mix that desire with time. Commitment, commitment, and more commitment. The commitment will stop you from just drifting day to day and getting nothing accomplished. Follow your passion but remember, what gets measured gets done.

3. Timestamp every goal, give yourself a time to start and a time to finish. Still finding it hard to get started? Then try this method. Each day for the next two weeks, pick a specific time and do one thing towards accomplishing your goals. Just one thing but be consistent. I promise you that if you commit and change your mindset towards accomplishing any task you have set for yourself you will be successful. Then when you look up one day, you are one step closer to turning that vision and those dreams into something tangible. But you have to commit to one small thing. It is called the compound effect. One small thing, then another, and before you know it, you have accomplished your goal.

4. Use the library to check out books or buy books by an author who has accomplished what you wish to achieve. They have done it and so can you. You just have to do it by taking one baby step at a time. Need a story? See how I got started in chapter fourteen. So, discover you, find your passion and purpose, and then take some action. One step at a time and it is possible with hard work you can be blessed beyond your wildest dreams. I love the quote by Tony Robbins, "If you want to be successful, find someone who has achieved the results you want and copy what they do and

you'll achieve the same results." Go ahead; the world is waiting for you and your ideas. And the most crucial part is, the world needs you. Trust me, there is someone that needs to hear your story, and you are the only one that can give it to them.

LESSON LEARNED

Who has done what you are trying to do? Find them and model their actions. When I started this book, I made all kinds of excuses as to why it would never happen. Excuses such as, no one would want to read anything I have written, no one would think anything I had to say would be important, and who do I think I am writing a book? I come from St. Matthews, South Carolina. But I chose to get started by writing a plan, then I started a paragraph here, and a paragraph there, and a funny thing began to happen. Ideas came to me like water in a stream, and I believe they did because of the commitment I made to myself and the goal I wrote down. I also just stopped listening to all the lies which were coming out of my head and went for what I truly wanted to do. You can do the same thing. Just one step at a time.

Reflective questions

1. What do you want to commit to? What is it that is stopping you?

2. What burning desire do you have that you are constantly putting out? Why are you scared of what people will say? When you are eighty five years old, none of that will matter. The only thing you will have is the feeling of regret that you didn't at least give your dreams a platform to live.

3. What are you good at that can change your life and turn your family's love around? Mine was just making the decision that I wanted to leave PE and become an eLearning expert. Commitment, even when I didn't want to do it. Even to the point of not doing some things you really want to do with your friends! Commitment!

4. What baby steps can you take just to get started? Is it writing a simple paragraph? Is it going to the library to check out a book or even just enrolling into a course? Is it just taking a piece of paper and writing down what you want to do?

Have a vision and desire, commit to that vision and desire, and take some action to accomplish that vision and desire, succeed and then repeat the steps for continual success.

"The first method for estimating the intelligence of a ruler is to look at the men he has around him." -
—Niccolo Machiavelli

Chapter Twelve

LOW SELF-ESTEEM

The first and best victory
IS TO CONQUER

"The first method for estimating the intelligence of a ruler
is to look at the men he has around him."

Niccolo Machiavelli

Remember this, you don't have to be everything to everybody and do everything. You just have to do what you were created to do. One of the issues I use to suffer from growing up was very low self-esteem because of how unintelligent I thought I was. There were friends of mine in school who while in class, would just get a topic and run with it. They just understood what was required to pass a particular section of the curriculum and I just didn't. It took me years to realize that all of us have multiple intelligence. We just have it in our own ways, deeply engrained within our own gifts. For instance, the same person who could grasp a particular part of the curriculum, maybe he or she couldn't catch a basketball and make a shot. Both acts took intelligence but different types of intelligence, and this is what I want you to see. No one person has the knowledge to do everything, but even more importantly, what you have to understand is that we have to find our blessing, our gifts, find out what we have to do, and run with that. Trust me, you do have it inside you, sometimes it just takes longer to manifest itself.

I personally think yes, it is intelligence, but even more importantly, I believe that it is all tied to confidence. To me, confidence is the ability to believe that you can accomplish a goal. The belief that you are smart enough to chart a path towards greatness within your area of expertise, not someone else's area of expertise for you, but yours, not your parent's vision for you but your vision for you. But of course, confidence can only make an appearance when you have carried out the work, and this involves an understanding of what type of skills or knowledge are required to complete a task. Learning the methodologies necessary to complete the tasks or the knowledge which is required to be successful is an ongoing process. One that can take an extended period of time to accomplish but only if you are ready for success. When you are seriously ready to move forward into the land of excellence, the land of confidence and belief in yourself.

Once you understand this, then I truly believe that it is important that you stop comparing yourself to everyone else, especially those people you consider friends. What we don't realize is that half the time people are only trying to show you who they want to be and not who they are. Everyone has issues in their lives. Everyone and I mean everyone.

Sometimes the magnitude and intensity of those issues we suffer are only magnified by what we feel or what we feel we should have accomplished compared to that of our colleagues or our so-called friends.

One example can be your friend, yep, your friend who uses social media to broadcast either how he or she is doing or how bad they feel about a particular situation instead of trying to find a constructive way of solving that issue of a lack of self-esteem or a lack of doubt.

When I was 22 years old, I was drafted by the LA Clippers of the NBA (then they were called the San Diego Clippers). When I was cut, I made up my mind that I had too much talent to waste and besides, I wanted to continue to play. The one thing I knew was that I didn't want to be involved in the system of continually trying out to make a team. So, I wanted a life now, and that is a decision that I look back on now, and I can honestly say that I have never regretted that decision. Ever! I had some friends who told me what they thought I should do and if they were me, they would do this or do that. I quickly realized that because they had no real awareness of my situation, they really couldn't inform me constructively. And the same for you, people are on the outside looking in. So instead of listening to them, I made up my mind that I would do what I thought was better for me.

So, what did I do? Well, I just left the country. Yep, I left the United States of America with no idea of what life held in store for me. However, one thing I do know and believe is that God has an amazing way of making things happen when you have a made up mind. I had no idea how I was going to leave and find a job playing basketball. Then the most wonderful thing happened. While sitting in Bobby Cremins' office one day, Coach Cremins made a phone call. He knew some people in Finland and within ten minutes, I had my first professional basketball job. Talk about quick. Man, I cannot tell you how happy I was. My dream was coming true; I think because first of all, I always believed something positive was going to happen, and I made sure I kept myself in an environment of success.

I am truly convinced that if you believe in a higher power, as I do, that it is possible to believe that good things are in your path. You have to just believe, and I wasn't wrong. Or even if you don't believe, then you have to find something deep inside of you to help you believe.

After spending two years in Finland I found myself back in the Coach's office again. This time with one of my dear friends, Charles Payton, who I had played with for one year at Appalachian State University. We had been speaking no more than twenty minutes when the phone rang. Again, that phone. The call was for Charles. He'd been on the phone for maybe five minutes when he leant over and asked me, "Boo (that was my nickname, his was Boo-Boo), hey man do you want to go and play basketball in England?" Well, within three days we were on a plane headed to England. Blessings will come your way if you are prepared for them and work each day with a purpose However, I think that the real key is that you are prepared for that chance when it appears. I really do believe this because I have seen these blessings appear in my life, especially when I was prepared. How was I prepared for a basketball job? Well, I worked out in the mornings by running, lifted weights after lunch and played basketball in the evening. Because of that one decision, where I gave myself permission to go ahead with my life and travel and not wait for something to happen for

me, and instead of listening to others who knew very little about how I really felt I tried to make something happen for me. What do I mean by this? Well, Bobby Cremins knew I wanted to play basketball in a different country because I was in his office every day telling him. If anyone could help me, I knew it would be him.

Charles knew I wanted to play because we discussed it all the time. Having played together, he knew the passion I had for the game and just how badly I wanted to play.

You have to put yourself on the spot or a place where the opportunity can find you. You have to stay ready. Stay ready at all times, ready to search and be prepared for that opportunity. I am telling you it will come if you first believe and then you do the things to help create the opportunity framework for your dreams to materialize. Because of those decisions, I now have two amazing children who have done things I think are amazing with their lives and a wife, Janis, who has been the foundation and architect of our lives.

I have a job where I am working with teachers and students to help educate them and better their lives. I am the first person in my direct family to go to university to get my BA and then a Masters in Education. Being prepared and looking for opportunities every day of my life. You see, once you know your why, searching and looking for opportunities is not a problem. You just have to be driven, driven to the point where you have to make something happen. You just have to make something happen; I refuse to accept anything else. I just refuse and so should you refuse to accept anything except what you really want.

I run camps helping teachers and students to use multimedia in their classrooms, along with being an author for Lynda.com and LinkedIn. This helps me to not only reach and help educate millions of educators, but in turn, the teachers are using the information learned from me to impact their students' lives. All because I started working on my gift. As a young boy, all I ever wanted to do, once I realised my gifts, was to play basketball, all I ever wanted in my life was to have an impact and change the world even though I had no idea how I wanted to do that at such a young age. I wanted to make more money and see the world. Does that take confidence, you bet it does? Why did I have confidence? Well, the main reason is because I spent years and years playing basketball and developing skills to the point that I was ready to compete against the best both physically and mentally.

I also knew in some way that it would be a gift that would help me in all facets of my life. I just knew it would. Sometimes as Dr. Martin Luther King said, "If you can't fly then run, if you can't run then walk, if you can't walk then crawl, but whatever you do, you have to keep moving forward." I think you have to choose how you want your life to turn out, and to be honest, sometimes you just have to go on blind faith and belief.

So, as I look at life, the one word that comes to mind is simply Priceless. So, do I look back and wonder what would have happened if I had stayed in the States and kept trying to make a path in the NBA?

I can honestly say, NO, I don't. I am right where I need to be, doing the things I need to do in order to help both my family and our society prosper. I can't and won't look back because today is all that I have and all that I can do anything about. Are you looking forward in your life and using your gifts to help you succeed? Or, are you just wondering day to day taking whatever life gives you, or are you living in your past? It is your choice and only yours. When you realize that it is all about how you are going to manage yourself and your gift, I mean when you really realize this, all you will want to do is to move forward.

However, sometime there will be times when you will need to ask someone and I believe that if you just try and see the problem from a different perspective by getting feedback from someone who is not very close to you, you may be surprised just how much you can learn.

From my experience, I think the problem with most of us is that we are in our own minds too much. Let me explain just what I mean. Each of us undergoes lots of the same types of experiences, but the negative part of that process is that we think we are the only ones who go through those experiences. I believe the key is to be able to understand what is real and what is not. If you are not careful, the mind can play tricks on you, such as telling you that you can't do something, or tell you that you are not good enough or even that you are not as good as your next-door neighbor. There used to be a slogan that the Army used for their commercials in the States "The mind is a terrible thing to waste." I agree totally.

Especially if you are spending your time believing that you are not good enough or sitting around complaining about how much the world owes you or even that it is not fair that Bob has all those wonderful possessions and such as a wonderful family and you don't. Have you ever thought that maybe if you wrote your goals down, wrote the steps to help you accomplish them, along with timestamps for their accomplishments, developed an I-won't-quit attitude and then started working toward accomplishing them, that your life would be better?

Please give it a try. But I really don't believe that you can accomplish your goals on your own. I think that our experiences are only really beneficial when they are shared with each other.

I don't know of anyone who has not needed someone else during their life journey to help them succeed. We need each other to be successful. It is just a fact.

So, from today, start looking around your neighborhood and see what types of programs are being run by others. For instance, government programs or programs from your local schools or libraries. Search the Internet for free tutorials to help you learn these skills that you feel are holding you back from reaching your goals, using sites like YouTube and Vimeo. I know that there are free resources at the library because when I was wondering how I was going to change my life from a PE teacher to an eLearning expert, all I had was the library.

I spent every single day in the library using the books, using the internet, and taking a standalone course on the internet to find out what the internet was really about. Man, I mean every day after work for at least an hour for one whole year. The only time I wasn't there was when it was closed on Sundays. I just had to figure out a way that I would learn and create to take advantage of any opportunity that came up in my school. I just wanted to take advantage of the opportunity in the lifetime of that opportunity.

At the time, I was working at the Grey Coat Hospital School in London as a PE teacher and had made the decision that I needed a life change. It just so happened that the Head of ICT at the time, Suzy Ralph, told me, before she told anyone else in school, that she was pregnant and was going to have time off. She knew how much I loved ICT and just casually mentioned to me that her job was going to be available. Remember about taking advantage of the opportunity in the lifetime of the opportunity?

Well, this was an opportunity that I saw that could possibly make a difference in my life, my family's lives, and to the students I was teaching.

So, one day, I was mentioning my dreams to a friend of mine, Ryan Elliot, and he said, "Renaldo I know a guy who has a laptop and wants to sell it. It has never been opened, and he'll sell it for £200. I tell you, blessing will chase you if you put yourself in a position to be successful. So, I bought the laptop. Then I had a thought. What was I going to do with this machine? Well, the answer came quickly enough. I knew that if you are going to learn anything you need to have a reason to learn. You also need to use what you have learned over and over again if you are going to retain the information. So, what better way of doing this than asking all the Head of departments in the school this simple question. If you had the opportunity to have a site on the internet or intranet and it could reflect what you are teaching, what would you have on it? I could not believe the response.

Every single department gave me their curriculum to use. What now I thought? Then I knew, I just knew, that I needed to take advantage of this opportunity. So I wrote a game plan on how to organize all the information. Then reality hit me like a ton of bricks. I didn't know what the heck I was doing. Then, as if by magic, I was covering a lesson one day in the library and while the students were completing their coursework, I decided to take a look at a few of the books. Lo and behold I found a book about the internet. I cannot begin to tell you just how right that moment semed. Everything just clicked. Why not use the library to learn how to use the internet and how to create interactive documents? That is how my career as an eLearning developer started. Simply by taking advantage of an opportunity when it appeared, staying in the moment, looking at all the possibilities, choosing one and just doing it.

Was the journey lonely? Darn right it was. The nights that I stayed up till three in the morning, and I tell you there were many of them, trying to get content to upload, trying to get one image to align to the left or even just trying to learn how to add and hide the table in a web page. Having my wife tell me that I was crazy and asking me, "What good is it doing you? You are not making any money". I had to stay focused and remember that it was my dream and most people will never understand your dreams.

You just have to make up in your mind that nothing is going to stop you. I only had two choices; I could continue living my life and be unhappy and unfulfilled or I could take advantage of the opportunity that had presented itself to me.

Phew, man, has it been worth it? Without a doubt. My decision has changed my family's life, my life, and just as important, I can impact the world every day with content that is both informative and engaging. And to top that off, I had the opportunity to teach my son for two years, and it was a phenomenal experience, all by staying ready and taking advantage of the opportunities that were presented to me.

LESSON LEARNED

I have learned that when opportunities come your way, you need to be prepared to take advantage of them. I have also worked out that sometimes even if you don't know how you are going to accomplish a goal, when it is presented to you don't say no, you just figure out a way to get it done. Think about it because it just might be the best opportunity you will get. You never know when opportunity will stick its wonderful head through the door, but when it does, tell it that you are ready to rock and roll.

Reflective questions

1. What opportunities are looking you right in your face but you can't see them because you are looking too hard?

2. What is that gift which every day you think of using but haven't had the guts to start using? Maybe you need to take the advice of the Nike slogan which says it best. "Just do it?"

3. By not pursuing your dreams and goals, who have you disadvantaged? What has your family not done because you haven't perused your goals? This is not a guilt trip question. Just a question to get you to thinking about how much impact your life has or could have on your family and the world.

4. Are you living someone else's journey? Maybe that parent who wants you to be a doctor? I believe that you have to live your own dreams, find your own happiness, and tackle every day that you have on this earth with purpose and desire. It is your choice. Why aren't you just doing it now?

Chapter Thirteen
A MOTHER'S LOVE

"A mother is the truest friend we have, when trials heavy and sudden fall upon us; when adversity takes the place of prosperity; when friends desert us; when trouble thickens around us, still will she cling to us, and endeavour by her kind precepts and counsels to dissipate the clouds of darkness, and cause peace to return to our hearts."

—Washington Irving

It would be impossible to write a book and not start where it all began, the foundation of my life and my brothers' and sisters' lives. The foundation that is Pernell 'Mud' Lawrence.

Throughout my life, I have been blessed to see and experience the life of a woman who continually blessed others and strived for greatness within herself, all while trying to raise seven children. From the first time I knew who I was as a person she has been there through good and bad. She has been the rock on which we all, my brothers and sisters, have been able to stand tall on and reach heights that none of us thought we would. Pernell 'Mud' Lawrence, our mother is that rock.

I have literally seen my mother give the shirt off her back to a woman in need. I have witnessed my mother take in kids who didn't have food to eat or a place to lay their heads. I have witnessed all of this, not for a day but all of my life. All my life, and it continues today. The amazing thing about her doing it all these years is that she wanted nothing in return except to know that she made someone else's life brighter and bearable. So, growing up, each day, I saw a woman who raised seven children and a whole neighborhood. A whole neighborhood. I have seen first-hand the respect that was given to her by grown men and women, as well as children of all ages. Mrs. Mud, they call her. I call her the servant leader, and I, like my brothers and sisters, have been blessed to have her as a constant source of inspiration in our lives.

Pernell 'Mud' Lawrence was born on December 4th, to Bosie and Rosa Caldwell. She was the oldest of the children and the one who helped raise the other children. Before Pernell was born, Rosa and Bosie Caldwell had lost two twins. I like to say that regardless of what tragic event has occurred in your life, God brings sunshine and treasures the next moment and Pernell's life has been a treasure to everyone she has come in contact with. Pernell has never been one to take fools likely, and she will voice her opinion whether you want to hear it or not.

There are many stories that I could tell about Mud, but the two that really resonate me with are firstly the story of her going back to school to get her high school diploma and secondly, her stopping smoking after forty years. One of the things always stressed by our mother in the household was that education was a fundamental part of our lives. I think this was very important to my mother because during the 40s and 50s, to have an education as an African American wasn't that common. But as my mother would tell me, sometimes "book smarts" was not all there was to being an educated person. Common sense plays a large part in how one conducts one's life.

Both of her parents had only a 3 to 4th-grade education, but I tell you what, both my grandparents had so much knowledge in terms of how to treat people and how to run a successful household, that I never noticed their lack of a formal education. My grandfather handled the finances and could keep financial records with the best of them. My grandmother knew her measurement and could cook and make anything that was required in terms of clothing. So, my grandparents were plentiful in terms of worldly education.

But Pernell wanted more for her children. She wanted to equip us with an education that no one could take from us. She always used to say to us, "Get an education, pay attention in class because what you learn there, no one could ever, ever take that away from you." This really holds true, although it was not always the way I thought about education.

As a child, Pernell used to get up around 4 am to 5 am every day, do her chores, and then make her way to school, walking up to six miles a day. Later on in her life, while I was in high school, we had a conversation that I remember as if it was yesterday. She said to me, after I voiced my opinion about the value of education , "Well, I'm going back to get my high school diploma." You see she had to stop her education at a young age because she was required to work at home to help her parents. She continued, "I have always felt that there was something missing from my life. I also couldn't ask you children to go to school, get an education, and I didn't have a diploma." Here was my mother, aged forty, telling me she was going back to school.

This had a tremendous impact on my life, so much so that I eventually got my BA from Appalachian State University and my Masters from St. Mary's University in London - all because of that conversation I had with my mother. You see, I took on the role of mentorship for my whole family. Now I was the one who could show them the way, show my younger brothers and sisters the value of having an education, and I could only do this by following in my mother's footsteps. And now, I have the opportunity to share my love of education with my students at the different schools I have taught in and the world through my courses at Lynda.com and LinkedIn Learning - all because of that one conversation with my mother.

So, I say to you, when you are talking to your children or anyone for that matter, be careful what you say because your conversation could change not only the person listening to you but the world. Just a small conversation could be the difference between someone having and developing confidence in themselves and finding their path in life. Just a simple conversation.

Another story about my mother that showed me the strength, love, and character of the woman was when she stopped smoking after thirty five years. Unbelievable. She went from smoking almost two packs a day to none. None! Later on in her life, I asked her why she stopped and her reply showed me the love, dedication and hopes she had for her children. What did she say? She said to me that the reason she quit was because, "I didn't want my children to grow up thinking that smoking was a good thing. Also, how could I ask you not to do something that I did right in front of you?" Man, I thought and think even to this day what a role model she is to all of us. I feel so proud and lucky to be born to a woman who understood that her actions in front of her children would impact them. And you know what?

I am now a firm believer Pernell's actions - going back to school to get her high school diploma and stopping smoking - had a huge impact on the way I raised my children. Having such an amazing role model there was no way I was going to ever let her down. And to this day, both consciously and unconsciously, my life is a product of the love, grace, dedication, and impact she showed to both her kids and her community. A priceless and dedicated community leader and an incredible human being. I know that Pernell had to make a choice a long time ago.

Pernell had to decide that she was going to give up on some of her dreams to ensure that her children could reach theirs. I use all the lessons I have learned from Pernell 'Mud' Lawrence to help me today to create my own path in life. All the lessons I learned from Pernell, I now use to help me raise my children. One statement Pernell used to say to me often was, "Never ever let what anyone say stop you from living your dreams. As long as you are not breaking the law or hurting anyone, follow your heart and ambitions. Never let other people's limitations define you." Still today, I can hear those words coming out of her mouth.

LESSON LEARNED

I believe that there is an ultimate price all of us must pay if we want true happiness. I mean happiness where it feels as though your heart is about to burst out of your chest. During my lifetime, I have been excited about getting stuff like presents, going back home from England to America to see Pernell and the rest of the family and just knowing that I will have time in the summer to just chill. But I can say to you right now, the biggest feeling of happiness I have ever felt other than when my children were born is the feeling of helping someone else in life. Just helping someone else live through their day, feel good about themselves, and understand that they are very important.

Although I believe that the feeling of wanting to help others is ingrained naturally in my soul, I think it got there through watching Pernell in her daily life. Just watching the love and care she took in helping other human beings when they didn't have any food, when they were struggling with money, and yes, even when they were struggling with their own self-esteem and morality.

How can you get that feeling? I honestly think you can get that feeling by helping your next neighbor, by opening the door for someone, by letting someone share their story with you and possibly their pain. But you have to practice. You have to look for a reason to practice and to be honest, create situations where you can open your heart to others. What do I mean?

Well, I just moved to a new school and didn't really know anyone there. As I have mentioned before, I am a very observant person, and so I look for situations to be nice and helpful. Within the school, there is a department that takes care of students' needs called Students Services. Because I walk through that area often, I noticed how busy they are constantly, so I took it upon myself to introduce myself to them. I know that every day all they do is to deal with students' and parents' issues. So, I make a conscious decision to always to stop by and say hello when I am in that area. Not a big deal I know, but one that I know they appreciate because the ladies have mentioned that not only do they appreciate it, but they also mentioned that no one else does that. No one. I find and create situations to be a blessing to others. Why? How could I not with Pernell as a role model? I have been blessed by my mother and it is my job to. No, it is my responsibility to make sure that I bless others.

Every day we walk by people and know nothing about their lives, even some of the people we work with daily. It takes nothing from you as an individual to smile and say hello. I work from the premise that if their lives are anything like mine they will have issues. A "hello" might sometimes be the only brightness I receive in a day. So, it is up to you and I to brighten someone else's day. Take the challenge today and make a difference in somebody's life. If we are going to make our world a better place, we have to. There is no choice.

Reflective Questions

1. How can you bless someone else today by saying something as simple as hello?

2. How do you know what you have in common with the next person unless you start a conversation?

3. How do you know if you don't speak to that person that the person is going through something you have already dealt with? You may help them to overcome adversity.

4. How can you create a situation where you can bless someone and not want a blessing in return?

5. Who can you talk to today who doesn't look like you that might just help shape your perspective on life for the better?

I truly believe that our wellbeing as human beings is predicated on how we interact with the next person, regardless of sex or age. You have a golden opportunity to change the world. One conversation at a time. Your life and your choice.

JUST A THOUGHT

Life has a way of ending too soon. We don't know when the end will come or how it will come. What a shame if our lives should end before we fulfil our goals, our hopes and dreams, and before we seize the opportunity to tell our nearest and dearest how much we love them.

Life is an amazing thing and you realize just how special it is when you have loved and lost a special one. We all have a special gift that we call life, and if we are honest, most of us daily take it for granted and can't wait for some of those days to end. End because we are having a bad day, end because we have a trip we are looking forward to and trust me, it happens to all of us, and there is nothing wrong with that.

But I believe that it is time we learned to stay in the moment, for the moment is all we have. We all have to live, love, express our feelings and sorrows, and help each other learn how to love the life we have.

So, I hope this book will help you understand that together we can change not only ourselves but the world.

Chapter Fourteen

FRIENDS

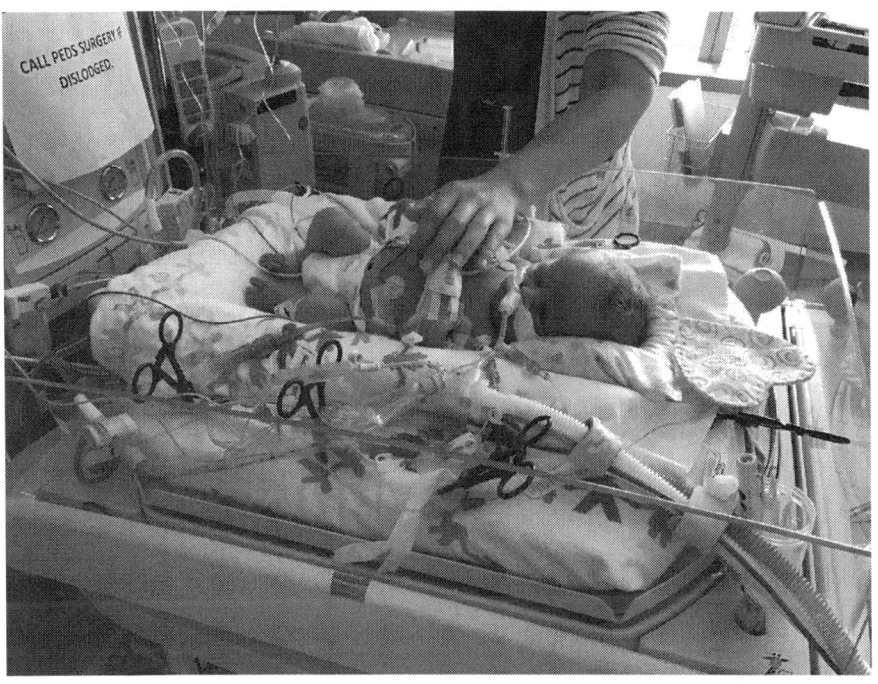

"The greatest gift of life is friendship, and I have received it."

—Hubert Humphrey

FRIENDSHIP – BONUS CHAPTER

Sometimes you are blessed beyond your wildest dreams. It is even more amazing when you didn't ever dream or think of the blessings that have been bestowed upon you.

THERE IS NOTHING better than the opportunity to meet different people from around the world. I am lucky that in my role as an Adobe Educational Leader, Apple Distinguished Educator, Microsoft Innovator, and Teacher Developer, I have met some of the most interesting and creative people in the world. But to me, the best part of meeting people is when you meet someone, and something just clicks. You find that you have a common bond and becoming friends just seems natural.

Well, one of my deepest friendship didn't exactly start off like that. Let me set the scene.

As an Adobe Educational Leader, we have the option of meeting as a group every year in a different part of the world. Sometimes we would meet in New York City, San Jose, California, or another city in the US or Europe.

Ever since I have been a member of the Adobe group, I have never missed one of these conferences because of the opportunity to learn what other educators are doing in their classrooms around the world. This has helped enhance my ability to be successful in my own classroom.

It has never ceased to amaze me how wonderfully talented these educators are. Meeting them yearly, regardless of how briefly, just fuels my soul. To me, it is creativity at its finest.

This particular summer, we all met in San Jose at one of its finest hotels. I arrived from England around 6 pm, so I was late for our first meeting. This wasn't a problem because this meeting was just a get together to say hello, meet new members, and say hello to old friends. When I arrived, it was as usual really nice to see everyone, and, as usual, I got the feeling of amazement. Amazement mainly because I have in some ways always wondered whether I actually belonged in this group of the outstanding educators.

Well, after I had said hello and met everyone, I decided it was time to go to bed, mainly because I had been traveling all day and was dog tired. eighteen hours at airports, on planes, and in cars will do that to you.

When I got to my room, I had a nice shower, took out my laptop, turned on the TV, and got into bed just to relax.

About an hour and a half later, I heard a card key unlocking the door. That was no surprise to me because we always have a roommate during our summer camps. I really love the rationale behind the reasoning of having a roommate. The opportunity you get to talk with your roommate is extremely beneficial for all three parties concerned.

Reasons being:
1. Each of the roommates is from a different part of the world, and the cultural differences are amazing. So not only do you get to know someone from another part of the world, you get the chance to learn how they teach, work with other teachers and you learn about their technological interests and specialisms.

2. Like Adobe, I believe that diversity enhances your ability to solve problems. It's generally recognised that people with different backgrounds, skills, attitudes, and experiences bring fresh ideas and perceptions.

When the door opened, there was a brief moment of silence because Dan, the guy who just walked, in was new to the group and was unsure of how things worked. Dan sat his bags down, looked at me, and then promptly told me that he had to make a phone call. I thought nothing about it and said, "OK, see you later."

It was only years later that Dan told me why he walked out so abruptly. You see, unbeknown to me, Dan had never really had meaningful contact with anyone who was not white, and I was black. As Dan would tell me years later, the one real contact he had was a student who was in his school and that student was mixed race.

The phone call that Dan made was to his mother. Dan called his mother to tell her that he had a roommate who was black and he really didn't know how to handle the situation. Dan's mom told him to just be himself and things would work out, but to just be careful.

For every year since that first meeting Dan and I have been roommates.

That was seven years ago and Dan is now one of my best friends ever. As a matter of fact, he is my permanent roommate at all the Adobe events. We laugh so much about that phone call and how he felt, and talk about how our relationship has grown. As a matter of fact, at the time of writing, Dan and his wife have just had a baby, and they thought enough of our relationship to name their baby after me.

One night after the events in 2017, while sitting in our room at the Adobe camp, Dan asked me to turn the TV down, he said that he had something serious to speak with me about. So, as he requested, I turned my full attention to him because by the tone of his voice I knew he was really serious.

Dan proceeded to tell me that he and his wife had talked about names for their baby over for the last three months and decided to give the baby my last name, Lawrence, which would serve as the child's middle name. As Dan said that to me, tears flowed from my eyes that I had brought so much value to his life through helping him grow as a man that the both of them just thought it was a natural fit.

Shock does not even begin to mention the strength of my emotions or how much pride and joy I felt at that moment.

Today, before my trip from San Jose to Chicago, I was lucky and blessed enough to get the opportunity to go by the hospital to see our little fellow. Again, what an emotional experience to see the little fellow in the small crib being taken care of by his nurse. The little guy had one of my names. At that moment, I thought of how lucky I was that God thought enough of me to put Dan and I together way back seven years ago as roommates. I believe that God makes no mistakes and as I think back over the years we have known each other, I thought I was the one who had grown from our relationship. God works in amazing ways.

So now I have another family to love and share experiences with. He makes no mistakes.

LESSONS LEARNED

You never know when a chance meeting will not only change your life but that of the individuals you meet. Just the opportunity when one person meets another. There is nothing better than the friendship of another human being. The ability to connect on a human level is second to none, especially if the connection is genuine. When you find people, who are for you and you are for them, life becomes an amazing adventure. Simply amazing.

You just might end up with a whole other family.

Reflection Questions

1. Who have you met that you feel a genuine connection to that could be beneficial to each of you?

2. Who do you see on a daily basis who you would want to make a positive connection with?

3. What opportunity is right in front of you that you could take advantage of that will help you be successful?

"If opportunity doesn't knock, build a door."
—Milton Berle

CONCLUSION

I know that in life, like you, I am special. The only problem with most of the world is that they need to continually have confirmation about how special they are. I personally believe that confirmation starts with you reaffirming or affirming who you are, who you wish to be and what you want out of your life. We all have choices, and I think that if we don't know who we are, then it is very difficult to get to where we wish to be. You see, as you journey through this big world, it is you that is responsible for you. No one else is responsible. People may help you advance in life, but ultimately, it all comes down to who you are and who you wish to become.

There will be trials and tribulations but if you look at them in the right way, that they are a way of making you stronger, then you will grow and become a stronger person. I have mentioned in this book many times about writing things down.

In Habakkuk 2:2-3 verse, it says, "Write the vision; make it plain on tablets, so he may run who reads it. For still the vision awaits its appointed time; it hastens to the end – it will not lie. If it seems slow, wait for it; it will surely come, it will not delay."

I believe that it is so critical that you write your goals and visions down so that you can see where you are going. When those trials and tribulations come, they won't be as shocking as they could be because you have your vision written down and it is right in front of you.

I wish you the best in your life. You are of a Royal Priesthood, gifted and blessed. Now all you have to do is to believe and walk in it.

Made in the USA
Lexington, KY
22 May 2018